John Wilson (Jack) Foster was born in east Belfast and educated at Annadale Grammar School and Queen's University, Belfast. A Fulbright scholarship took him to the University of Oregon, USA to earn his doctorate. He spent his teaching and research career at the University of British Columbia, Vancouver, Canada and has taught, researched or lectured at the University of Ulster, University of Toronto, National University of Ireland Maynooth, University of California Los Angeles, and the National University of Ireland Galway. He is a Fellow of the Royal Society of Canada.

IRELAND OUT OF ENGLAND

And Other Inconveniences

JOHN WILSON FOSTER

BELCOUVER PRESS

To the memories of William J.V. (Bill) Neill
and William Beattie (Bill) Smith

Scholars and gentlemen both

" ... if way to the Better there be,
it exacts a full look at the Worst"

THOMAS HARDY
In Tenebris II

LITERATURE AND CULTURE

Forces and Themes in Ulster Fiction (1974)
Fictions of the Irish Literary Revival: A Changeling Art (1987)
Colonial Consequences: Essays in Irish Literature and Culture (1991)
The Poet's Place: Essays in Ulster Literature and Society
    (co-ed. Gerald Dawe, 1991)
The Achievement of Seamus Heaney (1995)
The Nabob: A Tale of Ninety-Eight by Andrew James (ed., 2006)
The Cambridge Companion to the Irish Novel (ed. 2006)
Irish Novels 1890–1940: New Bearings in Culture and Fiction (2008)
Between Shadows: Modern Irish Writing and Culture (2009)
Midnight Again: The Wartime Letters of Helen Ramsey Turtle
    (ed. 2021)

POLITICS AND CULTURE

The Idea of the Union: Statements and Critiques (ed., 1995)
The Idea of the Union: Great Britain and Northern Ireland
    (co-ed. W.B. Smith, 2021)

SCIENCE AND NATURAL HISTORY

Nature in Ireland: A Scientific and Cultural History
    (co-ed. H.C.G. Chesney, 1997)
Recoveries: Neglected Episodes in Irish Cultural History 1860–1912
    (2002)
Pilgrims of the Air: The Passing of the Passenger Pigeons
    (2014; 2017)
The Space-Blue Chalcedony: Earth's Crises and the Tyler Bounty
    (2020)

TITANICA

The Titanic Complex (1997); rev., *Titanic: Culture and Calamity* (2016)
Titanic (ed., 1999)
A Better Boy: A Titanic Monologue (2017)
The Age of Titanic: Cross-Currents in Anglo-American Culture (2002);
    repr. as *Titanic and the Sceptre of Power* (Kindle, 2017)

Contents

Introduction

The essays and articles below were written between 2017 and 2023, in what we might call the immediate post-Brexit period of British and Irish history. They are reprinted in the order of their composition.[1] They were not written in hostility to the people or the everyday life of the Republic of Ireland where I've lived and made many friends. As a singer and songwriter, I was active in the folk revival of the late 1960s and early 1970s when a generous common purpose seemed to connect much of the youth of Northern Ireland, Irish Republic, Britain and North America. I sang at hootenannies and concerts in Belfast (and later in the coffee houses and at folk concerts when I moved to Oregon in the U.S.) and attended *fleadh cheoil* in the Republic. The music then seemed below (or above) party politics and was a happy and boisterous all-island affair.

I later lived in Dublin in the early 1970s and mingled as a hopeful literary critic with writers in McDaid's and the other buzzing writerly pubs. (I particularly remember a spirited exchange with an elderly but still bullish Liam O'Flaherty and the poet Hugh Maxton over perhaps too many pints). Socially, I preferred, on the whole, Dublin to Belfast, Southerners to Northerners. In my professional life as a literary scholar and critic, I have written sympathetically about more Catholic writers than Protestant. These preferences are now sadly beside the point. The IRA campaign of terror waged against unionists brought politics and citizenship to the fore and sidelined all else. Then the "culture war" of the 1980s and 1990s (between revisionists and traditionalists in the South and between nationalists and anti-nationalists in both North and South) also took its toll of my unsullied admiration for the South. I've maintained my friends in Dublin though I lost a few when I ticked Yes to Brexit. In the 2016 referendum I voted as a citizen of the UK rather than as a resident of Northern Ireland, since I identify as British and Irish in equal and inseverable measure. I chose the larger geopolitical context with its broader span of implication for my life.

Any hostility in the articles and essays is to the post-Brexit surge of exclusivist Irish nationalism across swathes of Irish society, including the so-called moderate nationalist political parties, and which harries unionists with its clamour for a border poll and predictions of unification. There had been some years of genuine respite and hope from the late-1990s after the IRA ceasefire, though the conflict *per se* didn't end. Rather, it changed register and became cultural-cum-political instead of paramilitary-cum-political (the Armalite and the ballot box as the clever, obnoxious republican slogan had it). This version of the conflict has been incomparably better for everyone's wellbeing, though the conflict is fought on its new terms just as earnestly and determinedly, though rather one-sidedly at present.

So I felt these essays and articles had to be written. They are reactive rather than pro-active, written in response to a newly invigorated and emboldened Irish nationalism determined, on multiplying fronts and from comprehensive quarters, to secure a united Ireland and wrest Northern Ireland and its pro-Union citizens from the United Kingdom. During the course of this renewed campaign, I have read or heard almost no sympathetic insights into post-1960s unionism or ordinary decent unionists by those seeking to absorb them in a united Ireland (or indeed by those in Great Britain who are on paper their allies). Hardly a siren song, then. Unionism apparently has simply to be cancelled. So most of these chapters are rejoinders to a nationalism largely too self-enamoured to bother explaining and justifying itself, lazily and self-righteously assuming that history (it used to be God) is on its side, so why bother explaining or justifying the inevitable (it used to be the ordained)?

Like most writers, I take pleasure in the craft of writing, yet have taken little pleasure in writing the magazine essays and newspaper articles printed below. My writing has been in the main inspired by admiration, curiosity, a sense of betterment, or celebration, but combating hostile political designs offers much less reward and self-improvement. Also, the subject of the articles and essays is uncongenial and the Northern Ireland crisis is taxing, corrosive and, if one is not careful, brutalising, in the correct use of that word. What can one expect, given that the energising tumult of the civil rights campaign of the late 1960s was followed by the terror and counter-terror campaigns - our own small-scale, vicious Thirty Years war. By contrast, my written appreciations of literature have been self-affirming - never more so than when I spent months reading, pondering and savouring the Bellaghy poet while writing *The Achievement of Seamus Heaney* (1995).

The problem is partly one of becoming implicated in the divisiveness of sectarianism, ethnic hostility and political fundamentalism. The brushstrokes become broader, the chances of having one's motives deliberately or unintentionally misconstrued greater, and the contentiousness of one's opinions likelier the closer one approaches the heart of the matter. A full look at the worst, to borrow the poet Thomas Hardy, makes the way to the better a risky undertaking. Under challenge, you begin to think and write in bold font. The alternative is to call for harmony and reconciliation. That seems the solution, especially if you see Northern Ireland's political predicament essentially one of ethnic tribalism and mutual religious prejudice, both of them in a regional vacuum. But alas the issue is conflicting constitutional demands and identities, each with geopolitical hinterlands. The latter invites red lines: but how to draw them while being alive to nuances and the legitimate wishes of those you disagree with?

I don't recall anyone I knew raising the question of the effect of

Brexit on the constitutional status of Northern Ireland or hearing any debates on the matter, North or South, during the campaign leading to the referendum. Brexit was a high-profile catalyst for a reinvigorated united Ireland campaign only in the post-Brexit years. Brexit was lambasted as a very bad thing by the government and commentariat of the Republic throughout the referendum campaign; after the vote Brexit suddenly became an opportunity to be warmly embraced. At that point I realised (since my special period of study was the Irish literary and Gaelic revivals, 1890s-1920s) that the new dynamics of nationalism were actually the old ones come again and are today increasingly determined and as orchestrated and multifaceted as they were in that earlier period.

But with this difference. In the earlier period there was a genuine and viable Irish nationalist desire to break with Britain in order to redress historical wrongs, achieve sovereignty and create a society as unlike Britain as possible. For decades nationalism succeeded, though at great material and immaterial cost. Since the 1960s, the world has interconnected more tightly, and the Republic has grown socially and culturally closer to Britain, despite Brexit and Ireland's cleaving to the EU. But politically it has endeavoured perversely to become more politically estranged from the bigger island. A united Ireland is the most symbolic way of attaining distance from Great Britain. But in the light of social and cultural reality, the idea of an independent united Ireland, with an annexed Northern Ireland as final proof of sovereignty and a total sundering from Britain, makes no sense and verges on hypocrisy or delusion on a national scale. Besides, I have seen in the Republic little genuine interest in, or knowledge of, Northern Ireland and its Catholic or Protestant inhabitants: its eyes are fixed on England. Northern Ireland is a pretext for the imagined solution to a quite different but carefully unacknowledged problem and which is the locus of the only way forward to peace and stability I can see and that I broach several times below.

That there is a full-blown debate in progress between unionists and nationalists about the shape of a new Ireland outside the United Kingdom is a nationalist figment that springs from this other, real problem - the relationship between the Republic and Great Britain. Northern Ireland is a proxy issue and the Republic is trying, apparently without self-awareness, to escape the gravitational pull of Britain. But it can't be done, with or without Northern Ireland, for the best talents of Ireland happily yield to that gravitational pull. It makes infinitely more sense for the Republic to acknowledge and then find ways of giving institutional expression to the inseverable intimacies between Great Britain and Ireland. This would mean the Republic turning its scrutiny inward and its gaze outward beyond the island instead of collectively, unanimously and endlessly gaslighting Northern Ireland unionists. I hope some of my inconvenient observations are inconvenient truths and ultimately helpful.

This is the only way forward I can see that can bridge the divide between northern nationalist and northern unionist, or perhaps one should helpfully and more accurately say northerners of a nationalist background and those of a unionist background. In any case, since friendships measure one's own nature, I always thought it perverse to regard "Some of my best friends are ..." as a self-mocking, boomeranging formula to rebut the charge of bigotry. I don't know precisely how many of my friends "of a nationalist background" are happy living in the United Kingdom, but I know some are. Others would prefer life in a 32-county Ireland, reunited with those they consider ethnic or cultural kin (and I suspect some of these would be happy in a UK to which the Republic was more closely aligned), but this has no bearing on the friendship or on religious background. The quarrel outside friendship is, or should be, between ideologies and constitutional aspirations, not religions unless in their secular and political outworkings.

And the quarrel should be conducted through competing forms of persuasion and certainly not through violent coercion which failed after thirty years of misery. But today, activist nationalism wants to cut out the middle man of persuasion and cut to the chase. This is apparently to be done through legal, political, economic and cultural machinations in disregard of the unionists' wishes to have the devolved Northern Ireland government up and running on a level playing field (which Brexit upset on the nationalist side and the NI Protocol on the unionist side) and to have the constitutional status quo maintained, and the republican campaign for a united Ireland suspended to give everyone breathing space.

Whatever repetition there is in the essays and articles stems from the reiterative demands of nationalism but also from the diversifying promotions of a Northern Ireland outside the UK. But I have tried to vary the reader's diet by taking note of the larger geopolitical landscape which Northern Ireland, the Republic, and Great Britain currently inhabit. There is an unfolding revolution on foot of multiculturalism and mass immigration that is both the result and engine of multiculturalism. The ensuing growth of home-grown and imported identity politics in race, ethnicity, religion, and gender is threatening the social cohesion of the English-speaking countries. Several of the essays below discuss these strains in Canada and the United States. The South of Ireland has appeared until recently to be immune from this loss of cohesion, to be an odd man out among Anglophone nations. The united Ireland campaign is premised on a firmly cohesive Irish nation, so cohesive that it can absorb almost a million unionists loyal to the UK and retain its cohesion; indeed, such absorption will, it's assumed, satisfy the century-old demands of the 1916 rebels and complete Irish nationhood through this "inevitable" process of final unification.

But the events in Israel of October 7, 2023 and the ensuing Israeli response have caused waves that have reached the shores even of Ireland and caused division on the streets of Dublin. The wider the Middle East conflict becomes, the deeper will be the divisions in the Republic of Ireland and other western societies. Partisans on the Palestinian side are unexpectedly active in the UK and US because of recent patterns of high-volume immigration, but in the Irish

Republic the governments have traditionally had radical reservations about Israel that unionists on the whole don't have. Moreover, this particular conflict has coincided with acute unrest at home. Recent immigration from non-Anglophone and non-European countries has had a destabilising impact on working-class Dublin that mirrors that in the UK but is more localised and eruptive. Both parts of Ireland have a long history of rioting. The November 2023 riots and looting in central Dublin, propelled by working-class, north-side anger, had echoes of the third act of Sean O'Casey's *The Plough and the Stars* (1926), set during the Easter 1916 rebellion. But O'Casey's "terrible state o' chassis" has new impulsion that perhaps derives from the riots in Seattle, Portland and other cities that followed the murder of George Floyd in Minneapolis in 2020. Canada, Britain and Ireland are especially vulnerable to the effects of events in the United States and there is an element of imitative responses to events at home. If Seamus Heaney indeed remarked that the world through identity politics was becoming Ulsterised, it is no less true that Ireland is receiving the disruptive imprint of what is happening in the big world. All the more reason, surely, to suspend a united Ireland campaign, to step back and take rational stock. Time for us all to pull together until such times as minds and hearts are free and safe to change.

NORTHERN IRELAND, UK
2017–2021
BRITISH COLUMBIA, CANADA
2021–2023

1   Many of the essays and articles appeared in *The Irish Times*, *Belfast Telegraph*, *Briefings for Britain*, *Irish Pages*, *Conservative Woman*, *News Letter* (Belfast), *The Critic* or *Dublin Review of Books*. I thank Professor Liam Kennedy for permitting me to reproduce his article-length reply in the *Belfast Telegraph* to my article questioning his proposal for a Museum of the Troubles in the city.

God's Away on Business

"The ship is sinking," rasps downbeat Tom Waits, but "God's away on business. Business". His ominous tidings come to mind when I ponder the state of the Union on this side of the water.

Once more, these are worrying days for those who wish to remain UK citizens. Pan-nationalism has suddenly returned, perhaps because the illusion that it had gone away was maintained by all-island EU membership. The ship may not be sinking but there's a noticeable list and the crew is decidedly skeleton.

In the past forty or fifty years abandoning ship – while not abandoning belief in the Union – has been a feature of frontline unionism, even if it was mostly executed in an orderly and muted fashion. The nobility and gentry exited first, with remnants staying at the tiller until the early Years of Disgrace, which I prefer to call the Troubles. Some, like Lord Londonderry in the 1920s, had like Othello done the state some service. As first Minister of Education, for example, he wished to introduce integrated education into the new Northern Ireland but was thwarted by the usual clerical suspects.

But the nobility were never as important in Northern Ireland as the linenocracy. A handful of linen families wove this part of the world into being and the most die-hard northern Shinner is the beneficiary of their expertise and at times business genius. The industrial families ran not just the economy but also municipal politics, Unionism and then Northern Ireland. There were among them, of course, philistines and bigots, Gradgrinds out of Dickens' novel, *Hard Times*. And the deep mutual distrust and dislike on the island between North and South, nationalist and unionist, Catholic and Protestant, meant that the reluctance of many northern Catholics to acknowledge the legitimacy of the young state accompanied an ungenerous anti-Catholicism by those in charge.

But there was a streak of liberalism, too, in early Northern Irish unionism and the Scottish historian, Professor Graham Walker reminds us how progressive was someone like John Miller Andrews (minister 1921–40, 2nd Prime Minister 1940–43), with his "step-by-step" doctrine, which meant keeping abreast of progressive UK legislation. The 1947 Butler Education Act (which applied to Northern Ireland the 1944 mainland Act) liberated the cleverer among the working class (Catholic and Protestant) and indirectly (and ironically) made possible the civil rights movement. Arguably it eventually benefited on balance Ulster Catholics more than Ulster Protestants.

The city fathers leavened their business and the power it brought with a strong sense of civic obligation and philanthropy, something that has all but died out among us. No Lady Pirrie, then no Royal Victoria Hospital.

Then industry collapsed after World War Two, a war in which members of the linenocracy distinguished themselves. Some of the industrial families adapted and even prospered, but they largely withdrew from political life. The big names echo no longer in the chambers of government. Their descendants are away on business.

And no one could have blamed business people, prominent and small alike, for ducking their heads below the parapet during the IRA onslaught and the loyalist backlash. The Sinn Féin project, after all, was to render Northern Ireland economically impotent and businesses were thus "legitimate targets".[1] But times have changed, though the metal shutters still on our shop fronts are ugly reminders of how unsure we are of that. It would be refreshing to hear robust, articulate and generous promotions of the Union from successful people of the world, even if in a private capacity. With one or two exceptions, successful male actors from Northern Ireland enjoying a high profile in Great Britain embrace the idea of unification, quite possibly for unreferenced reasons of career profit.

With a few politicised exceptions, the professionals – the solicitors, barristers and medicos – have likewise decided against lending their verbal and intellectual skills in promotion of a polity without which their professional lives would be sea-changed. A foreign visitor would have the absurd impression that whether or not Northern Ireland remains in the Union is for those in professions and commerce a fairly neutral issue.

Our two universities, publicly funded for the most part, house our greatest concentration of resident educated minds. Until fairly recently, those minds regarded themselves as belonging to "gown", aloof from "town" and its politics. But in an era in which "impact", "outreach" and "output" are the criteria by which academics live or die, curiously these do not extend to engaging with the home body politic. Business elsewhere is detaining academics and administrators; they are preoccupied with racism and gender issues imported from the U.S. and GB.

Yet there is an unspoken prevailing cultural assumption even among our writers. "Be advised," Seamus Heaney told his London editors in his *Open Letter* in verse (1983), "my passport's green./No glass of ours was ever raised/To toast The Queen". Were you to read a Northern Irish poet addressing his Dublin editor with "Be advised/My passport's blue", the slim volume would jolt from your hand. One sentiment is permissible, laudable, even thrilling. The other is naff, infra dig, counter-poetic. Yet under other circumstances, the silent among us, writers or no, will smartly produce our blue passports. As, indeed, Seamus Heaney himself would have done when he was a youth. As it turns out, he had a British passport before he had an Irish one; he acquired one early in order to go on the pilgrimage to Lourdes, as he told Mark Carruthers in interview (*Alternative Ulsters*, 2015). To have revealed this in

1983 would have lessened the public force of what is (considering that the bombs were exploding and the bullets livid) a relatively good-natured exercise in public identity politics; his blatant, doggerel-like rhymes qualify any earnestness. Nevertheless, the poet's rehabilitation of his nationalist identity is unabashed. Also, the earlier passport is an oblique reminder that middle-class and educated Catholic alienation from post-war Northern Ireland did not begin in earnest until the 1970s.[2] Such pro-Union silence has enabled hardline nationalists to assume that unionism is a door banging with diminished confidence, to borrow the Glengormley poet Derek Mahon.

The stupefaction that Cuchulain the Ulster hero once suffered was called "the great enchantment" by Standish James O'Grady, the scholar who re-introduced the Iron Age hero to the Irish. O'Grady thought the phrase appropriate to political Ireland in 1903, "under a spell and its will paralysed." I'm tempted to reach for the parallel myself when I consider political unionism. But it's both simpler and more complicated than paralysis of the will.

Simpler because silence and absence are reversible: cut short your business and take care of your vital interests at home.

But the silence of tolerance is normally a virtue. It is what made our deeply divided society work in the main, as my social anthropology teacher at Queen's University Belfast, Rosemary Harris, explained in her classic *Prejudice and Tolerance in Ulster* (1972). "Whatever you say, say nothing" has been a *modus vivendi* with us. But as Heaney knew, it has its limits and there comes a time to speak out, ideally with the forceful respectfulness of that poet.

But with most everyone who could make a difference away on business, we are left with those minding the Union store who (with notable exceptions) have neither the historical and cultural knowledge nor eloquence to earn our confidence, however courageous they can be. This has allowed the cartoonish reduction of unionist culture to bonfires, flags and marches.

Unionist culture is bigger than bonfires, bigger than Sinn Féin, bigger than Ireland. One of my objections to a united Ireland is that it would return me from the larger to the smaller. After a spell on an island in the Gaeltacht in the 1930s, the major writer Sean O'Faolain caught cabin fever. "Any sensible man naturally goes from smaller to larger islands. And ends up with continents, which are also islands within the popular definition."

I love Dublin but if London is my capital how could I shrink my civic horizons? If I am a distant offspring of the British Empire (whatever one thinks of the Empire) how could I dwindle myself to Ourselves Alone? I suspect the Dublin intelligentsia feel the same way because they too are integrated into the culture of the archipelago, though they won't or daren't say so. That is why they are panicked over Brexit: fear of being culturally separated from the UK.

And with all due respect, EU membership is not the answer to our Irish dilemma. (Though we must not have a hard border again.) The European Union project is to shrink Europe to a stifling unitary bureaucracy. Anyone who believes Brexit means by definition turning one's back on European or Irish cultures, is, frankly, a dunce. Rather, it's the desire for elbow room and fresh air.

An impelling vision of the Union would reset the relationship between the autonomy of devolved administration and the rights and responsibilities of UK citizenship. The latter should trump the former when it matters. As it is, the DUP, refusing the "step-by-step" doctrine, are maintaining social planks in their platform that drive a wedge between us and the rest of the UK. They might prove the Achilles Heel of the Union. I for one would welcome a return to the "step-by-step" doctrine. The DUP stand against same-sex marriage and abortion reform impairs the Union and alienates the unionist young into the bargain.

"It's all over. It's all over," chants Waits in "God's Away on Business". It's not yet, of course, where the Union is concerned. But I'd like to see those away on business coming back and telling us why not. Is it too much to ask for the Union to be reaffirmed with an informed sense of the past and not a little passion? (2017)

1 The journalist Ben Lowry believes that the IRA campaign was designed in a broader span "to terrorise unionists out of politics" and that the 1983 murder of Edgar Graham, the Queen's University law lecturer and rising unionist politician, achieved just such a chilling result (*News Letter*, December 9, 2023).

2 Malachi O'Doherty in 2019 (*Belfast Telegraph*, November 11) unearthed a quote from Heaney in 1968 in which the poet feared that "the old polarisation" in Northern Ireland (i.e. in his father's time) was returning; O'Doherty remarks that this implied that before 1968 Northern Ireland was not polarised, which contradicts the idea that Northern Ireland had been polarised from the word go.

An Angry Wind –
Maud Gonne and Violence

Beyond dispute are Maud Gonne's energy, initiative, charisma, beauty and height. At an eye-catching six feet or more (6'5" is the tallest hero-worshipping exaggerated estimate I've read), she was tall but not pointlessly tall, tall beyond utility as Martin Amis claimed of Nicholson Baker. Her height, once she got into her stride, as it were, usefully gave her a leg up in a pre-radio, pre-Pathe News, pre-TV era of street politics, of milling crowds, marches, riots, stumps and open-air platforms. She was always visible and early came to relish and exploit that visibility, a literal high profile.

Adrian Frazier's new book, *The Adulterous Muse: Maud Gonne, Lucien Millevoye and W.B. Yeats* (2016), recreates for me, for the first time, and perhaps without that intention, the sheer physicality of the woman, endlessly on the move from house to house, office to office, country to country (and lover to lover, it turns out), cutting a swathe, it seems like, through men shorter than herself and often under her large feet, getting between her and the mirage of a free independent Irish republic on the horizon. She seems to have turned up everywhere in turbulent Ireland from the Land League to the Emergency, a larger-than-life Zelig but far from content with a minor role, instead elbowing her way to centre stage even when she wasn't invited (which she usually was).

Frazier's portrait of Gonne in its essential commotion is very different from my previous impression of her as a figure whose actions, such as trying to hurl the little streets upon the great, nonetheless had the static quality of heraldry. For Yeats her beauty was a tightened bow and out of nature, unique for her own day. "She lived in storm and strife," Yeats may write ("That the Night Come", 1912), but her "high and solitary and most stern" beauty is the frozen image that prevails. The women she was compared to, Helen of Troy, Joan of Arc, Pallas Athene, or embodied, Cathleen ni Houlihan, Deirdre and the Countess Cathleen, reinforced for me this heraldic and essentially symbolic condition in which I came to think of her, suspending my moral and even political judgement. Her photographs are to me of a handsome and impressive rather than beautiful woman, but that is no doubt because standards of beauty change, and in any case her handsomeness is in harness with symbolism rather than sexual attraction which always implies the promise of movement. In the photographs she is always posing; that seemed true even when she was on stage; apparently as Cathleen ni Houlihan she addressed the audience in studious and stately fashion and ignored the other characters.

I had remembered Mary Colum as a sharp-eyed memoirist but going back to her *Life and the Dream* (1947) I find a boundlessly admiring portrait of Gonne that admits no reservation, a portrait unmoving in its perfection, despite her memory of Gonne's "Protean personality moving on various planes". Colum's last sighting of her is as an elderly woman at College Green addressing the usual assembly in a familiar tableau and described by a writer friend, as though she were a monument, as the most beautiful ruin in Ireland.

The blurb describes Frazier's *The Adulterous Muse* as "a captivating book" and if that means merely that it is a page-turner or entertains the reader, then the blurb is right. Certainly Frazier unravels the fascinating political intrigues and conspiracies Gonne apparently relished as well as the secretiveness (though mostly the compartmentalisation, as it turns out), of much of her personal life. But more seriously this is a liberating rather than captivating book. It liberates us from the Yeatsian image of Gonne most of us have lived with – springs her from the extended and dutiful footnote she inhabited – and gives us instead the autobiographical fiction she herself wrote and inhabited and the real narrative behind that. It gives us the information by which the reader can take the measure of this, all-things-considered, deplorably influential woman; a major theme of the book is the error of underestimating the political influence Gonne exerted.

Frazier's chief contribution is to shrink Yeats in Gonne's life and to detail the extent and nature of her political affiliations and actions in France, of which Yeats and her own followers (some of them blind followers) were largely ignorant. As a result, Gonne is liberated (though her shade may regret this) from the Yeats oeuvre to become a larger, more complex and more dangerous figure certainly than I realised. Refreshingly, Frazier calls his subject "Maud Gonne" throughout, instead of by her first name, in the manner of biographies of women by admiring female critics or condescending male critics. Frazier is squaring up to a formidable historical figure.

It would be a mistake to say that she emerges a more rounded figure: her compartmentalisation means her portrait is more like a Cubist depiction, of intersecting planes more violent than Colum implies. The republicanism she embraced, with the surrogate monarchism and soul-mysticism of the Celtic Revival thrown in, we already know about. But what I hadn't really registered was the ruthlessness of that republicanism she eagerly flaunted with a threatening sexual charisma (readily shaming men for their lack of manliness if they weren't as extremist as she) and incited others to put into practice. Nor was I aware of her ideologically unsavoury French bedfellows, literally and metaphorically. The gist of the French connection is accounted for in Nancy Cardozo's *Maud Gonne: Lucky Eyes and a High Heart* (1979) but Frazier is much more negatively judgemental in the matter.

Alongside our ignorance of the nature and extent of that connection, Yeats's image of her has seemed to pre-empt any moral judgement of this woman's views and actions. Their relationship was highly complex, as Frazier demonstrates (to some extent following Gonne scholar Deirdre Toomey in the matter of sex), occasionally having recourse to some elementary Freudianism which conveniently accords with the interpretation of dreams Gonne and Yeats went in for. After all, Yeats admitted that the woman had caused him heartache ("she filled my days/With misery"), that she abused her class and position by preaching violence "to ignorant men", and that she was an inciter of hatred. Yet, oddly, he blamed those who followed her (who lacked courage) rather than her (who didn't) and we seem to have followed his cue.

For Yeats she occupied a different order of being from mere violence in the real world and so was unaccountable in the ordinary (i.e., moral) way. "No Second Troy" (1908) consists of four questions that are rhetorical only in the sense that they are not answered in the poem and *are* themselves the poem. But they are not rhetorical in so far as they are answered by implication. Why should I blame her? You shouldn't. What could have made her peaceful? Nothing. How could she have been otherwise than she is? She couldn't. Was there another Troy for her to burn? No. Similarly, the famous question in "Man and the Echo" (1938) – "Did that play of mine, etc.?. . ." – is not rhetorical in so far as the question is simply unanswerable, though the poet has tried night after night to make it so he says. These are quarrels of a kind with himself (out of which he is making poetry) and which he contrasted to rhetoric which is a quarrel with others.

But we needn't accept Yeats's special or intensely personal pleading (powerful and eloquent though it be) except as a figure in his auto-mythography. And Yeats's familiar and scrupulous broadcast of pronouns ("her", "this man", "that woman", "certain men", etc.), by which he anonymises in the service of legend and drama, authorises us, as it were, to turn to the historical Gonne instead, which Frazier has done.

In this biography of Gonne up until 1916, neither Yeats nor John MacBride is the chief man, lover and influence in Gonne's life but instead Lucien Millevoye, a French politician. (This reconfiguration should of course have its effect on Yeats studies themselves.) Being Yeats's muse was for most of Gonne's career a sideline, while she regretted marrying the prudish, violent, drunken (if courageous) MacBride almost as soon as the ink was dry on the marriage certificate. In Frazier's account, it was Millevoye, whom she met in France in 1887, who gave aim and objective to Gonne's vague political energies. He came to maturity with a smouldering sense of grievance over the humiliation of the defeat of France in the Franco-Prussian War of 1870 and the loss of Alsace-Lorraine. Since he was, as Frazier deems him, a "proto-Nazi", it is hard not to think of the later German corporal smouldering with resentment over the humiliation of the Treaty of Versailles. Millevoye threw himself into seeking to overthrow the French government in favour of a right-wing Catholic Bonapartist regime spearheaded by General Boulanger.

Gonne was to become Millevoye's helpmeet in the causes of regaining Alsace Lorraine and restoring France to glory, in return for which he would help her in the cause of driving England out of Ireland. He professed to loathe England (because England had vanquished Napoleon) as much she did, though she was in fact an Englishwoman. It does not matter that it may have been only in hindsight (when she published her memoir, *A Servant of the Queen*, 1938) that she thought General Boulanger was insufficiently ruthless to lead a French political revolution: that shows that even in her seventies she prized ruthlessness above the gallantry and charm she saw in Boulanger when they met. Her own boldness initially stretched to smuggling proposals from the Boulangist party to St Petersburg that would damage English diplomatic interests, and this apparently generated a thirst for conspiracy, recklessness and treason which she happily slaked for the rest of her life.

Gonne has Millevoye tell her: "At times, the genius of a nation incarnates itself in a man" and the political corollary of that: "outstanding genius alone gives the right to rule despotically. The greatness of nations depends on their willingness to recognise this". Hence Napoleon's France, hence hopefully Boulanger's France (hence Hitler's Germany). The logical polity ensuing is what Frazier calls "plebiscitary dictatorship". Before long, Gonne saw herself as the candidate incarnation, but of Ireland not France. Yeats's poems must surely have encouraged her in this self-promotion.

Despite her English birth and family, with some Irish admixture, she took to referring to the Irish as "us" and "our race". We might call this identity theft nowadays, and Irishness has been a popular identity to thieve. In *A Servant of the Queen*, Millevoye's belief is repeated in an Irish context: the "national soul" (always a dangerous figment) "may incarnate itself temporarily in individuals from any class, for the spirit bloweth where it listeth", and the reference to class may have been meant to pre-empt any disqualification of herself based on her own moneyed English social status. When Frazier has Yeats criticising her for consorting with the mob rather than working on more rarefied projects with the few, like him, she manages in her retort to have it both ways: "Willie I have always told you I am the voice, the soul of the *crowd*". And so *A Servant of the Queen* has modest observations like these, almost as refrains: "great cheers were raised when they recognised me"; "The hall was packed as we went on the platform and great cheers were raised for Maud Gonne"; "I as the guest of honour"; "I was at the height of my popularity in France", and so on. There are several episodes in the memoir of minor as well as major contests and she always makes sure she comes out on top, particularly if the competition is English.

The greatest recognition came through seditious and revolutionary views. At one time she teamed up with James Connolly to instruct tenants in time of want to steal the landlords' cattle and sheep. Lady Gregory, Frazier reminds us, asked Yeats to restrain her from encouraging robbery, knowing that should Gonne go to prison for incitement to crime she would "gain by it the notoriety she wants", hence her reckless outlawry. (Later, Gonne got some private revenge by attributing Yeats's turn from nationalist activism to mere art for art's sake to Gregory's influence.) Many contemporaries saw Gonne's long love affair with notoriety as a primary motive but Yeats's Gonne, a beautiful and lofty Olympian, has long ago eclipsed them. So too has Gonne's own "auto-mythification", a phrase Frazier borrows from Anna Magny. This required a severe rearrangement and blue-pencilling of the life, both at the time and afterwards in memoir (she "ravelled her own story" – Yeats). Even during the fornication with Millevoye, and after, his wife is erased; her two children by her lover are unknown to Yeats and others in Ireland; in her telling in 1938 neither lover nor children are acknowledged as such. (Her sexual affairs don't bother me in the least; I am merely pointing out how in her self-portraiture she was parsimonious with the truth.) In the memoir, only French episodes that suggest a parallel between France and Ireland are related, and the murkier aspects of the French right are avoided.

Some of these omissions in life and letters are for understandable reasons of reputation and even legality since in France and Ireland in those days an unmarried mother would have paid the price of social dereliction and suffered loss of custody. When MacBride discovered his bride's past he was shocked irrevocably. Yeats's mythography was proof against similar personal damage and if anything, in Frazier's telling, strengthened his idea of their higher spiritual marriage.

The one thing Gonne was not coy or evasive about was the need for violence against England. She was wedded to that idea more than to any man. Even given the hard times that were in it in late Victorian and Edwardian Ireland (those inhuman evictions!), and the understandable conviction that parliamentarism was failing Ireland, her addiction to violence was deplorable, the more so because, as the *New York Times* once observed (quoted by Frazier), she was protected by her sex. Frazier is but the messenger in this regard: we need only return to her own words.

I had not read *A Servant of the Queen* for thirty-odd years but when I opened it after reading Frazier, I found it, while still lively and insightful (she is a good writer), exasperating and chilling in equal measure. How had I been so blasé about it when I was teaching Irish literature? One reason is Yeats; the other is now obvious to me: the Provisional IRA campaign 1969-1994, bringing the past horrifically into the present, had not yet irrevocably ended my academic, detached tolerance for bloodshed in the service of Irish nationhood. To Gonne, Parnell had failed because he had repudiated violence. (She was hardy likely to impugn him on grounds of an adulterous private life.) Thereafter, she never discouraged anyone who wished to plant dynamite in the cause of Ireland. She preferred men ("heroic men") who did so in the House of Commons to those who were merely MPs in the same cause. And those who chose violence could set their own limits: "it was absurd to say that any Irishman, *whatever he did*, had committed a crime against England or against civilisation", she declared. (My italics.)

She disagreed entirely with the Fenian John O'Leary (he of the "noble head", in Yeats's phrase) who had said that there are things a man must not do to save a nation. One thing that an Irish republican should certainly do is assassinate holders of high English office, she thought. And not just once, as unfortunately (from her perspective) had happened with the killing of Lord Frederick Cavendish and Thomas Henry Burke in Phoenix Park: every English king and every instrument of the state below him should be shot "one after the other". It was "continuity" of select assassination that is required, in her opinion. This amounts to republican jihadism: it is total guerrilla warfare Gonne advocates, even in 1938 – and in a book, moreover, published in England by an English publisher (Victor Gollancz) and republished in 1974 (in the midst of the IRA onslaught in Northern Ireland)! Gonne's reputation has been the beneficiary of the peculiar moral bracketing off of Irish terrorism and terrorists from the usual civilised standards of judgement. Yet here she is, delighted to meet one James Tully, renowned for shooting landlords without compunction, looking gratefully into his "dreamy grey eyes" and wishing Lord Clanrickarde could receive a bullet from "the mild-eyed assassin".

Gonne's anti-Englishness amounted to a monomania which hindered a coherent political belief system, even if she'd had the intellectual equipment to formulate one. In essence hers was a lethal cocktail of cod Celticism and ruthless physical-force advocacy. Still, it sponsored a variety of subtended worthy causes – eviction of tenants, Land League demands, prisoners' rights, the Boers, tenement children, workers' rights, civil disruption. Many of these were legitimate and just, and her energy was admirable; but always the recommendation of "most violent ways" (Yeats) alienated the non-violent. She was proud of the fact that she never indulged in self-analysis (which might of course have included ethical self-examination) so it is left to us to supply her political philosophy. Frazier explores its strands: the Anglophobia, spiritualism, anti-Semitism and Nazism beginning as Millevoye's proto-Nazism and becoming the real thing during the Second World War. As late as March 1938 (this is outside Frazier's time-frame), when ostensibly weighing the respective merits of Soviet communism and German fascism, she prefers, at much greater length, to find English polity inferior to both. She is contemptuous of Jewish money power but even more contemptuous of the British empire. And in 1938, she claims that Eire, grown flabby, could learn from Stalinism and Hitlerism.

Some biographers, for example Margaret Ward in *Maud Gonne: Ireland's Joan of Arc* (1990), have seen Gonne as a pioneering feminist. And Gonne did champion the rights of women under carefully chosen circumstances. But can feminism co-exist with fanatical nationalism? For Ward, Gonne's apparently can, for Gonne's feminism consists chiefly of "her insistence on women's rightful place within the heart of the nationalist movement"; Ward tells us Gonne's eyes would go cold with hatred when she mentioned England, that her hatred of Britain was inveterate, her republicanism unyielding.

The women's organisation Gonne founded was *Inghinidhe na hÉireann* (Daughters of Ireland) but surely it can't be called a feminist body – was it not a women's auxiliary nationalist movement? And can true feminism be a branch plant of a predominantly male supra-gender movement, and a violent one at that? And yet, when on those occasions Gonne was denied the comfort of her assumed Irish nationalist identity and was at bay, as she was during the bitter proceedings of divorce from the Catholic republican hero John MacBride in 1905, Frazier believes she fought her corner as a New Woman of the time during which she attacked marriage from a feminist perspective. (He is also alert to others of her virtues.) Alas, she rarely found herself outside the vicious circle of physical-force republicanism where her feminism might have breathed and developed.

Yet surely an Irish nationalist feminist might have explored avenues of communication with unionist feminists on the island north and south? But I see no evidence that she ever subordinated her Anglophobic republicanism to the cause of feminism in any thought-out way. Now that I mention it, where *are* northern unionists, female or male, in Gonne's world? For her and other republicans, northerners seem to have been satisfactorily represented by Alice Milligan, Ethna Carbery (Anna Johnston) and AE (George Russell), all nationalists. Looking back, it is amazing that most northerners – unionists – were simply invisible. Yeats deliberately ignored them because he found them distasteful but at least as a Sligoman he knew they existed and thought they were best left to their own unpleasant philistine and materialist devices. What on earth did people like Gonne think industrialised northerners were going to do when the mirage of a separatist republican island began to reify into a likely reality? Like many, John MacBride when he wrote to John Devoy in May 1914 thought of them as "Home Rule bluffers". The reality when it transpired delivered a shock from which southerners have never recovered. Gonne of course when the time came was oblivious and continued to blow like an angry wind; she was a member of the Anti-Partition League but that was simply pro forma stuff, a reflex affiliation from a lifelong irreconcilable.

I am grateful to Frazier not only for rousing me from my contented slumber in the matter of Gonne, but also for sending me back to Yeats's poetry with a refreshed appreciation of her ubiquity there and the origins of that very real misery that he said filled his days. (2017)

Beachheads and Wool

Deputy Adams was seemingly precise in his statistics when he addressed Dáil Éireann on April 6. In the Republic of Ireland, since 2011, those speaking the Irish language daily outside the school gates have declined in numbers by 4.4%. Those speaking Irish even inside the Gaeltacht have shrunk by 11%. He delicately omitted the percentage of the population actually speaking the language daily: 1.8%.

Whereas the government strategy of 2010 aimed over twenty years to increase the number of Irish speakers from 1.66 million to 2 million and daily speakers from 83,000 to 250,000, the strategy has been for Deputy Adams "an unmitigated flop"; government policy has been, he alleges, "an utter failure".

Bear in mind that the overwhelming majority in the Republic of Ireland are Irish patriots of Catholic background. Bear in mind that Irish is enshrined in the Irish constitution and is an official language of the state. Bear in mind that the Dublin government spends a thousand million euro annually on education in Irish, as Dennis Kennedy in these pages recently reminded us.[1] Anyone from outside the jurisdiction other than Deputy Adams (who is outside the jurisdiction when he is not Gerry Adams TD) would draw the obvious conclusion. Most Irish do not wish to speak Irish.

But not only do Deputy Adams and his party refuse to draw this conclusion: they wish to see the Irish government redouble its efforts and, in effect, impose Irish on an unenthusiastic population. And they wish to plant the troubled narrative of official Irish in the Republic here in Northern Ireland where the soil has even less nutriment than south of the border. If I may quote James Joyce: "That takes the solitary, unique, and, if I may so, *recherché* biscuit".

Those like myself engaged positively in Irish literature and culture find the decline of Irish sad. Irish indirectly contributed to the glory of J.M. Synge's English prose, and directly to the nobility of the Blasket Islands peasant memoirs about which I've written.[2] But Sinn Féin's language platform challenges our sympathy. It does so because it politicises the indigenous language of the island and links it inextricably to their goal of a united Ireland. A referendum on a united Ireland and an Irish Language Act (Northern Ireland) are two of their three main planks in their election platform and they are tongue-and-grooved.

I always thought the self-imposed task of my late friend Aodán Mac Póilin of Ultacht Trust was noble: courteously, knowledgeably, and entertainingly to promote the viability of Irish (a language he loved) unshackled to any political agenda. Open the avenues but let it find its way. The opposing reality is that the Irish language is one of the four pillars of Irish separatist identity erected in the two decades that led to the partition of the island of Ireland and to the creation of the Irish Free State. The Gaelic language. The Catholic religion. A de-anglicised culture. A republican government. The first three of these are on the ropes. The church is not essential to Sinn Féin republicanism, but language and culture apparently are.

Where language is concerned, Sinn Féin are trying to rewind history and might yet succeed in Ulster by political mesmerism and cultural blackmail.[3] It will take these, for the Republic is an English-speaking nation and its government is probably relishing the advantageous prospect of being the only EU Anglophone nation after Brexit.

If the Sinn Féin push for an Irish Language Act which would be in inverse proportion to the linguistic reality of Northern Ireland, that is because they are not interested in reality; they are interested in, indeed fixated upon, a political destination. The essential and defining purpose of Sinn Féin is to achieve a united Ireland. After all, they share their other political planks with one party or another in Ireland. If there were any doubts that the Irish language is being politically weaponised, then surely the recent march by what the sympathetic BBC called "Thousands of Irish language activists" should dispel them. Amidst their placards and flags, "Organisers of the march and rally say that an act has to be central to any political settlement." "Central" no less - language and politics now publicly inseparable.

In terms of what is good for the native tongue, the Irish language front is regrettable and even the Dublin-based journalist Ann Marie Hourihane has described the Irish language as "the nationalists' weapon of choice" (*The Times*, February 15, 2018). It may begin with street signs but through an Irish Language Act is bound to progress to much else. What we are talking about is public culture reassignment, likely to be rapid in Northern Ireland. "In the Republic," writes Hourihane, "almost a hundred years have been spent on a regime of compulsory Irish, bilingual road signs, civil servants who have to be able to limp through public business using a travesty of Irish, and a lot of politicians who can start and end a speech in Irish while being unable to answer a simple question in that language. ... In the South Irish has been used to exclude non-Irish speakers from official jobs, and from feeling entirely Irish. ..." After a century of promotion, 1.8% of the southern population speak the Irish language daily; that figure would be considerably lower in Northern Ireland. "The Irish language", writes Hourihane, "has indeed been weaponised – by republicans, for generations".

The mechanism affixed to the bow of the Sinn Féin icebreaker is called Equality, Respect and Protection. But everyone in Northern Ireland is already equally free to learn Irish and speak it. Or Mandarin. Or Polish. Already Irish is well represented in official Assembly documentation and on the ground is an elective second or third language for many. But that Irish should be made co-equal with English in the courts, administration, commerce, education and place-naming of Northern Ireland is a fantastic demand.

Besides, when Deputy Adams notoriously stabled equality in a Trojan horse, the word was instantly demeaned.[4]

Yes, Irish has been disrespected by unionists but for understandable if regrettable reasons. Were Irish uncoupled from republicanism, the disrespect would shrink. But I must say that cultural respect was in scant supply on Sinn Féin's side for three decades after 1970.

If unionists are cynical and unaccommodating about what they might otherwise be sympathetic to, Sinn Féin must glance into the looking-glass.

Nor does the Irish language need protecting. Nobody is seeking to quell its current use. I'm afraid that in the hands of the activists "protection" of the language is actually "projection" of the language. In their recent report, the Council of Europe, a human rights organisation, has nonetheless taken on board the absurd idea that an Irish Language Act is a human rights matter. Sinn Féin and the rest of us know that talk of "language rights of persons belonging to a national minority" has no sensible bearing on Northern Irish reality.

As Dennis Kennedy reminded us before the report appeared: "there is no non-English speaking minority disadvantaged by their use of English in daily dealings with various public authorities and the community at large".

The language activists try another tack. The Irish language "is part of our shared heritage". Yes and no. Of course our place-names and our syntax are often Irish in origin and these are to be relished. Just as many Canadian and American place-names are of Native Indian origin; yet no province or state is attempting yet to make an Indigenous language the co-equal of English, athough in any case the sheer numbers of Indigenous languages would make that an impossibility. The literature I study often has an Irish language dimension or hinterland. But the speaking of Irish in daily life and in transaction with official bodies – no, that was never my heritage. William Butler Yeats because he grew up in what became the Irish Free State was able to say: "Gaelic is my national language, but it is not my mother tongue". I haven't formulated a way of claiming even the first of these and I'm afraid Sinn Féin aborted my attempt many years ago.

There are, of course, unionists and Protestants who learn to speak or write in Irish. They have been doing so for a hundred and fifty years. Indeed, the Gaelic Revival of the late nineteenth and early twentieth century was steered by such enthusiasts, often Church of Ireland adherents in the south: Douglas Hyde formed the Gaelic League in 1893. My friend Aodán Mac Póilin was particularly warm on the topic of enthusiastic Ulster Presbyterian Gaelic-speakers of the nineteenth century. But back then, it was culture that was at stake, not constitutional politics.

But after the turbulent decade of the 1920s, that enthusiasm waned. Even before that, in 1915, Douglas Hyde, later to be the first President of Eire, resigned from the Presidency when he watched the League's politicisation. The kindly, self-identifying northern unionists and Protestants who not only advocate support for the language (who could object?) but also assure us there are no political strings attached may prove, I'm afraid, cat's-paws, unless of course they would be happy enjoying the language in a Sinn Féin-dominated united Ireland.

Sinn Féin surely must know that an Irish Language Act would not be in the best interests of the living language or of communal relations. But that is not its point; its point is to ready a firing platform closer to the target. Sinn Féin from the start more than a century ago have been catastrophists, not reformists, thriving amid breakdown and Sean O'Casey's "chassis", believing that their goal is to be achieved opportunistically through breakdown, sudden irruptions, and, periodically, physical violence.

But since the Belfast Agreement they have also become erosionists, seeking to erode unionist opposition steadily and piecemeal, each time establishing a beach-head further inland. An ILA is a beach-head very much worth establishing, perhaps indeed the most valuable of all.

If we look farther afield we might see why an Irish Language Act would be a plum in the lap of Sinn Féin. The St Andrews Agreement (2006) promised an Irish Language Act "reflecting on the experience of Wales and Ireland". We know the Southern Irish experience and it is hardly reassuring. And the differences between Wales and Northern Ireland are so stark that the proposed reflection is a foolish thing. Wales is not contiguous with a larger jurisdiction already practising the Welsh language and culture and with historic designs on the current Welsh principality. The chief proponents of the Welsh language are not tirelessly working for (and threatening) separation from the jurisdiction and seeing Welsh as the iconic medium of its political work.

To discover a context for the political understanding of language conceived of as the definition and badge of separatism, it might be better to consider Quebec, a province of a nation that the most politically active in the province would prefer not to belong to.

The Quebec Question dates from the very same period as the Ulster Question – the early seventeenth century. Quebec was historically a Catholic province inside a predominantly Protestant Canada and this added to the troubling cultural differences of ethnicity and language that created what Prime Minister Pierre Elliott Trudeau in 1970 called "social unease". That unease deepened into violence and Trudeau had to face down the terrorist threat of the FLQ (Quebec Liberation Front), active between 1963 and 1970. A core belief of the FLQ was the equation between Québécois (Quebec French) and the province's thwarted nationhood. Of the four "legitimate" targets announced by the FLQ in 1963, three involved the French language. They rejected the "colonial language", English.

The Canadian government had already addressed the province's social unease when the Royal Commission on Bilingualism and Biculturalism (1968) resulted in the Official Languages Act (1969), making French equal with English in all federal government services and in the courts. But this did not satisfy the FLQ nor did it satisfy the growing separatist Parti Québécois. Unilaterally through the province's Official Language Act (1974), Quebec became unilingual (officially French only). After decades of political agitation, having lost two sovereignty referenda (border polls) in 1980 and 1995, Quebec resorted to a successful programme of extracting political concessions from the federal government (Quebec has its own immigration policy and makes its own trade arrangements) and enacting language laws aimed at culturally de-anglicising the province. The result is that for all intents and purposes Quebec is a separate nation nominally inside the Canadian Federation. Indeed, Quebec Bill 96, which was enacted in 2022 and concerns the French language, begins: "The purpose of this Act is to affirm that the only official language of Québec is French. It also affirms that French is the common language of the Québec nation". The federal government amazingly did not question this use of the word "nation". There was no need for a third referendum since virtual nationhood has been achieved chiefly via the French language.

Language is regarded as central to Quebec's cultural and political identity. Quebec separatists believe what David E. Hurst recently wrote: "The assigning of names is the beginning of nation building". In Quebec, official language police (OQLF) patrol the towns and cities seeking out violations. In 2016 a Quebec City restaurant was censured for including "grilled cheese sandwich" on its menu instead of "sandwich de fromage fondu". Signs are measured to ensure the correct ratio of linguistic proportion. In this part of the world, minority language consciousness can often breed intolerance.[5]

In Northern Ireland, of course, the question concerns bilingualism, not unilingualism. But bilingualism is itself a sticky issue. It is not just a case of French on the cornflake packages (all food products must be bilingually labelled.) It involves fully bilingual central government services and courts, of course, but also the encouragement of lower tiers of government to offer bilingual services – in Northern Ireland that would be city and borough councils, public libraries, museums, hospitals, etc. Then there is publicly funded educational instruction in both languages where one language is in a minority condition. Irish speakers in Northern Ireland could claim perpetual minority rights and demand Irish-medium schools throughout the province. The situation in the workplace (proportional hiring and promotion?), in businesses and on the street and in the countryside (signage and information) will be distinctly contentious.

Canada is a vast and rich country that can afford cultural extravagances. Official bilingualism would beggar Northern Ireland while sowing division. And even in Canada, after almost a half century of official bilingualism, just 17% of the Canadian population can speak both languages. Through multiculturalism, official French-English bilingualism in most of Canada now looks silly. The affluent Chinese immigrants of Richmond B.C., a city adjoining Vancouver (who compose 50% of the population) largely ignore both riders of the official tandem bike and conduct their businesses in Chinese only. The Chinese know that by keeping their language they keep their separate identity – and multiculturalism ironically requires them to do so! In the city of Surrey, also adjoining Vancouver, Punjabi is spoken by 30% of the population (of a 50% visible minority population). Indeed, Punjabi is the third most spoken language in Canada and is now regarded as the third language of the Canadian parliament. In Surrey, South Asia is alive and well. Language policies and laws that don't reflect daily reality are political, not pragmatic.

Why, then, would we contemplate an official English-Gaelic bilingualism when even in Northern Ireland multiculturalism on the ground has made it an anachronism even before the fact? Incomparably more Polish is spoken in the province than Irish and this will become ever more evident, despite Brexit. But Sinn Féin like the Parti Québécois are driven and hidebound by ideology.

When my Vancouver friend speaks her fluent Parisian French in Montreal where she lives, she is answered irritably in Québécois-accented English. The message is clear. She is not *pure laine* (pure wool), the old Quebec term for those regarded as genuinely French-Canadian. It is not speaking French that matters, it is being Québécois. The language is a means of communication but also a badge of identity and instrument of exclusion. Québécois is a nativist possession and there are degrees of (thwarted) authentic nationality as there are in Northern Ireland.

The St Andrews obligation remains and must somehow be met. But there are various kinds of formal and informal encouragements of the Irish language that can be practised without bankrupting the treasury, inconveniencing and alienating the population, and advancing a political party's project to undo Northern Ireland. But an Irish Language Act is not one of them. (2017/2023)

1   Dennis Kennedy, *Belfast Telegraph*, February 17, 2017.
2   I discuss Synge and the Blasket Islands memoirists in my book, *Fictions of the Irish Literary Revival: A Changeling Art* (1987; 1993).
3   And so it has proved. The Identity and Language (Northern Ireland) Act (2022) is an Act of the Parliament of the United Kingdom; it was promised to Sinn Féin if they returned to Stormont Assembly, which they had brought to its knees when they walked out. The word "Identity" in the title of the Act suggests the cultural and political implications. Belfast City Council has started vigorously to implement the Act. (2023)
4   That is what lies behind Gerry Adams' statement that "equality" is the "Trojan horse of the entire republican strategy" and how they will get "the [unionist] bastards" (*The Guardian*, November 25, 2014).
5   From autumn 2024, Canadian students from outside Quebec who enrol in any of the three English-speaking universities will face a doubling of tuition fees; this is to deter such students and advance the de-Anglicising programme.

Coming clean on the Lie of the Land

The legal challenge to the UK Government on the circumstances by which a border poll can be called broadens the front on which the campaign for a unified Ireland is being waged. The plaintiff was accompanied in a Belfast court by Fianna Fáil Senator Mark Daly, author of *Uniting Ireland and Its People in Peace and Prosperity*, a report feverishly detailed in its imagining of a unified Irish society.

Like that of the Queen's University human rights professor who anticipates a "profound dialogue" and "pluralist conversation" on the way to unification, the sky in Senator Daly's world is of a different colour from that in Sinn Féin's, if I can steal from Norm in *Cheers*. Both surely know that Sinn Féin is the pack-leader in pursuit of an overnight unified island and unlikely ever to accept the role of the pacemaking rabbit. Senator Daly is no doubt a thoughtfully sincere man, but he would find Sinn Féin a formidable obstacle to island amity. On the constitutional issue, Sinn Féin do not "do" dialogue, or conversation. That might, after all, expose the cracks through which the light gets in, to borrow Leonard Cohen. So better dogma than debate.

Instead, the inevitability of Irish unity is magical thinking, like Hamlet's belief that thinking doth make it so. Democrats should robustly reject what in theology is called teleology – the idea that events are designed to unfold towards a pre-determined conclusion.

But the predestined nature of a sovereign, 32-county Irish republic was born with the party. The Easter 1916 proclamation was intended to short-circuit the tedium of reform, persuasion, compromise and consent and cut violently to history's chase.

The current campaign keeps the faith. In 2009, Justice Richard Humphries entitled his book *Countdown to Unity* and, in an afterthought gesture to the exchange of opinion, subtitled it *Debating Irish Reunification*. The title makes it clear that the only debate referred to by the subtitle is to the hows not the wherefores of unification. Justice Humphries is quoted by Senator Daly throughout. This one-two of magic and reason, inevitability and possibility, is a feature of Irish republicanism beyond Sinn Féin's party walls. The plot-spoiler first sentence of the Daly Report is: "Ireland needs to prepare for a united Ireland."

The premise of the campaign is that at the behest of 19% of the Northern Ireland population who told the Queen's University/University of Ulster Life and Times Survey in 2016 that they wished to live in a united Ireland, the 66% who said they didn't should about-turn and march into an all-Ireland Republic.

They should forgo participation in a 65 million-strong society to join a (at best) guardedly hospitable nation of four-and-a-half million and swap London for Dublin as their capital. Dublin is a great city and Irish artistic culture a marvellous thing that I have spent my career studying. Even so, one of us should have gone to Specsavers.

Unionists are assured by Senator Daly that their British identity would be "protected" and "cherished" in a unified Ireland. If you need protecting, why go there? Yes, like the way the Anglo-Irish and their culture were protected? Memo to nationalist authors of manifestos of persuasion/coercion: lose the word "cherish", which began its Orwellian career in the Easter 1916 Proclamation.)

Sinn Féin also has promised us (though they are really speaking to those doughty architects of east Belfast bonfires) that they will accommodate our British identity in their united Ireland. Said the spider to the fly.

May I cut to the chase myself? From my quiver of reasons why I don't wish to live in an independent, unified Ireland, let me pluck merely one. Ninety-six percent of primary schools over the border are owned by and under the patronage of religious denominations, 90 percent of them owned and run by the Catholic Church. Very reassuring that, to secular and Protestant unionists. Irish Catholicism may no longer be of the head; but it is still in the viscera of the body politic and body cultural.

Amid the rising tide of international theocracy and the retreat of secularism and humanism, how likely am I to agree to accept even its relatively mild Irish backwater?

Those who campaign for a united Ireland should think twice. They seem to have no idea that the current Republic would have to reinvent itself so extensively to resemble secular and Protestant-shaped Britain that a united Ireland would be virtually pointless.

Neither the current nor envisaged public-policy Republic could possibly accommodate my British identity. It simply doesn't have the cultural storage space.

Which brings me to another report which has, indeed, thought twice. It is entitled *Coming Clean: Preparing for the Archipelago*, and its premise is that the united Ireland campaigners are looking through the wrong end of their binoculars.

It pursues the logic of Senator Daly's unpursued recommendation that to encourage the unifying of Ireland, "there is a need to recognise the inherent British identity on the island of Ireland as a whole".

If Brexit has stirred Irish nationalists, *Coming Clean* suggests it is because it has exposed the extent to which Irish society and culture are inextricably entangled with the UK's. Brexit is showing how closeness to Britain since 1922 has underpinned Ireland's sense of independence. After Brexit, what then for Ireland? Inside the belly of the EU whale.

The report reminds us of the constant interaction between the islands – free movement of people (a cosy two-member Schengen Area), a common labour pool, the UK market for Irish products, the passage of Irish goods across Britain to the Continent – on balance significantly to the greater benefit of the Irish than the English. It quotes recent headlines from the *Irish Times*: "Brexit burns Ireland's British bridge to EU markets". "Brexit may lead to later abortions for Irish women". "Brexit could decimate Ireland's horse racing industry". Even as mere headlines, these speak economic and cultural volumes.

These Brexit headaches for Ireland flag the bilateral intimacy of the two societies, underwritten historically by the often shared pain of experience, for which the Great War can stand as a noble monument.

It is arguable, we are told, that the economic logic of Brexit is Irish co-withdrawal from the EU, as Ray Bassett, the former Irish ambassador to Canada, has recommended.[1] Since Ireland is rightly proud of its advanced information technology, we could call it ExIt.ie.

The mutuality of popular culture goes without saying, but the report says it. English soccer is a huge and intrinsic component of Irish culture. The most watched programme on TV3? *Coronation Street*. The streets of Dublin were empty when Prince Charles married Diana – those caught without a TV were glued to shop windows.

It is on the whole an asymmetrical relationship. I remember the poet James Simmons' mischievous couplet from 30 years ago: "Why are the TV aerials in Dublin so high?/To eavesdrop on England, that's why!"

Much of the high culture of the south, as the report notes, comes from Europe and the United States, but chiefly from the UK. Those celebrated Irish professors in Oxford and Cambridge know it very well, as do the brilliant commentators in Irish newspapers who enjoy their privileged two-passport lives, while jealously guarding the single-passport lives of their fellow citizens.

Why not, the report asks, come clean and become a participant rather than eavesdropper in the wider culture of the archipelago?

The best of Ireland's writing is already a proud part of the canon of British literature. Ireland could become a net cultural contributor, the report claims, if it overcame the retro Little Irelandism that Sinn Féin promotes. And, instead of the southern Irish regarding unionists as enemies, the report recommends seeing them, in a radical change, as cultural point men on the archipelago during the reset time the Republic will need after Brexit, perhaps an over-optimistic take.

The run of the unity argument, the report concludes, is awkwardly uphill. Instead of talking about the British identity inside a unified Ireland, it would answer us better to speak of the Irish identity inside a more closely knit, post-Brexit archipelago. That identity would hardly need protecting, because it can well look after itself – and is already rightly cherished everywhere.

The post-Brexit onus is greater on nationalists to think North and east than on unionists to think South. Unionists need to promote the archipelago less than nationalists need to acknowledge it.

Coming Clean declares that not only is unification not inevitable, but its advocates repress the decades-old lie of the land.[2] (2017)

---

1   Dr Bassett considers the matter further in his book, *Ireland and the EU Post Brexit* (2020); the relevant chapter is reprinted in contracted form in *The Idea of the Union: Great Britain and Northern Ireland* (eds. John Wilson Foster and William Beattie Smith, 2021). (2023)
2   Some commentators contacted me, wanting a copy of this fictional report, which gave me small gratification by suggesting its plausibility. (2023)

A National Museum of the Troubles?

I so admire my colleague and friend Professor Liam Kennedy, the Queen's University, Belfast economic historian, that I dedicated to him my 2009 book of essays, *Between Shadows: Modern Irish Writing and Culture*. But on the idea of a Museum of the "Troubles" we are poles apart.[1] "Troubles" is in scare quotes because I reluctantly use that identifier, originally applied to years of vicious two-sided violence down south in the early-20th century. Like the "Emergency" (World War Two), it is a southern Irish euphemism; it has a soft funereal ring to it (as though a whole nation, doffing the hat, was saying "Sorry for our troubles") just as the Easter "Rising" (instead of rebellion) gave that insurrection a religious veneer – not at all unpleasing to the ear but somehow inappropriately comforting and muffling the often atrocious reality. "The Troubles" also implies a continuity in time and in space, thus imputing a unity of experience between the two regions of the island. Instead, borrowing a phrase from Menorcan history, I'm tempted to call our three decades of unjustifiable violence (1969–1998) the Years of Disgrace. So the proposal for a National Museum of the Years of Disgrace staggers me. In certain respects, we need to learn how to disown, not "own", the Troubles.

The premise of the proposal is that the Troubles are over and thus a fit subject for retrospect and also for profit ("export earner" in Professor Kennedy's phrase) and entertainment ("visitor attraction").

If only. Our conflict has entered a new, cultural phase while we are still at loggerheads politically, which puts into question the actuality of reconciliation, the history lesson the museum would apparently teach. Indeed, if the campaign for an imminent united Ireland is ramped up, we will regress.

Even today, if reconciliation were proclaimed, the divisions in our society would give the lie to that claim. There is self-segregation even at the educated levels and still only about 15% of our registered marriages are "mixed". So what have we yet to teach the outside world about harmony? Is a non-violent, but fragile and contentious political co-existence enough? In turn, a museum would belie our day-to-day rubbing along. We are a society in progress in Northern Ireland and hearteningly so. A Troubles museum would by definition petrify our differences. Besides, many of us suffer from "Troubles fatigue" and the thought of being immersed in it all again would deter many of us from buying a ticket to our recent inglorious past.

Museums in divided societies work only when history can be turned into "heritage", which nowadays means shareable history. We are a long way away from that where the Years of Disgrace are concerned. Shared suffering through profound constitutional division is not enough. I'm afraid the offence of those thirty years is too deep and raw for business consultants to remove with an entertaining money-spinner.

Titanic Belfast is the model for what is envisioned as an even bigger museum. But it took a century for the tragedy of *Titanic* to become a Belfast visitor attraction. When Michael McCaughan and I were first publishing essays on *Titanic* in the 1990s, we were alone in Northern Ireland where, because of sectarian interpretations, silence and suspicion surrounded the ship and its fate. But for *Titanic*, history did eventually lend itself to heritage. And it did so because there was much that was in the ship's memory that we could all take retroactive pride in – we once built great ships. "She was all right when she left Belfast," as the local T-shirt boasts.

A locally-themed visitor attraction must have pride as its

motivation. What is there to be proud of in our Years of Disgrace? There were, of course, gleams in the darkness - the bravery and dedication of firefighters, doctors, nurses, peace-making men of the cloth, anti-violence politicians. Unlikely, alas, to be the stars of the proposed museum.

The chief lesson of any commemoration of the conflict should be the wickedness of gratuitous violence - hardly the stuff of visitor attraction.

That leaves the tourists. Titanic Belfast is not primarily about tragedy: it is about a world-famous event with glamour amid the tragedy. I hope it is self-delusion to think that our vicious little war is, or should be, of global fame. As for glamour of a kind, I can think only of the legend of Bobby Sands – and that is hotly contested.

Because of the glamour of greatness, heroism and America, Titanic Belfast is not really what is called "dark tourism", in which the places or occasions of tragedy or horror are revisited literally or virtually. Black taxi tours of the Belfast neighbourhoods of conflict are a form of dark tourism and I for one have doubts about their morality.

On a more serious scale, Holocaust museums are possible because the cruelty and the suffering are one-sided. Rightly, they do not afford equal space to Nazi justifications of their behaviour. Only a Nazi could be offended in such museums.

But in the proposed museum, the voices of the violent would have to be heard. That will pose difficulties that will, in my own small experience in this matter, prove insuperable.

As sure as gun's iron, every display case, every voice-over, every virtual link, every material object, every caption, every "site-specific" history will be scrutinised and probably contested. Once, funded museums could operate without public input and oversight. No longer.

The proposed museum would approach international foundations and the EU for funding. They will demand the fair-mindedness and intellectual integrity that Professor Kennedy assumes will be on tap. He himself is one of the fairest-minded scholars it has been my privilege to know, but he is a rare bird in that.

Besides, fair-mindedness when it comes to violence in a divided society often translates as parity of culpability, which I for one reject, though certain others do not, itself a divisive factor.

Then there are our politicians, whose parties and councils have to be consulted and petitioned for funding. I co-researched and co-wrote with the local historian and author Allison Murphy the permanent Belfast City Hall exhibition on the history and culture of the city. Three hundred and fifty years went almost swimmingly. And then we came to 1969. It became apparent that a narrative of the three following decades acceptable to the committees of all the political parties was a mirage.

Our solution was a Reflection Room, displaying only heartbreaking statements by those who had suffered pain and loss. To me it was, in any case, preferable to an endlessly challenged story of who did what to whom – the Mobius Strip of whataboutery that we tread endlessly in Northern Ireland. Our inspirations were *Lost Lives: The Stories of the Men, Women and Children Who Died as a Result of the Northern Ireland Troubles* (1999, perhaps the saddest book in the English language), certain moving poems by Belfast poet Michael Longley, and the Reflection Room of the early RMS *Titanic* artefact exhibitions, devised by the late George Tulloch, CEO of RMS Titanic Inc., who had a touch of the poet.

The proposed museum could circumvent the contentiousness of the Years of Disgrace only by replicating the total complex reality. Virtual reality and digital technology encourage this illusion. The Years of Disgrace were a moral event, or they were nothing.

Professor Kennedy's vision of the digital museum threatens to re-create virtually (in both senses) the entire conflict. Among other things, visitors could "tune into significant events", including "killings, bombings". McGurk's Bar could be virtually rebuilt, obviously to revisit the atrocity. Are other atrocities to be retrieved by the visitor? La Mon? The Shankill Butchers? There are half-forgotten and obscene atrocities that haunt me to this day and I doubt if digital revisiting would exorcise their dark spirit.

It seems to me to be an invitation either to nightmare or to history emptied of its flesh-and-blood reality. The medium would be the message: we could certainly learn much from the museum, but we would also be there to have a good time, to enjoy using interactively the marvellous gadgetry that shrinks the world and retrieves a past that was horrible, but not so horrible in controlled simulation.

The lure of amusement, I'm afraid, is hardwired into the digital screen technology of visitor attractions. And pair that with the certainty that the museum would have to centre-stage the violence, the malign heart of the "Troubles".

The inevitable temptation is that of trivial pursuit. The website LoveBelfast beckons to me: "Come and experience Belfast's thrilling new escape room adventure, TITANIC: THE FINAL HOUR, one of Timescape's live escape games".

There are many existing resources for trying to understand the conflict, including the Public Record Office of Northern Ireland, the Linenhall Library and the CAIN archive. There is a display in the Ulster Museum and there are tours of the peace walls and murals. Falls Community Council is curating an exhibition in the former St Comgall's school of the conflict's impact on the neighbourhood. These are localised, discreet, even tentative representations of those 30 years, which is the way it should be. A "mega-project" of the kind proposed would institutionalise the Years of Disgrace and, because it would be a "National Museum", establish them as the central inheritance of two generations and the dominant cultural heritage of the past.[2]

Visit these diverse resources by all means. And read Liam Kennedy's brilliant book, *Unhappy the Land: The Most Oppressed People Ever, the Irish?* (2016).[3] But give a thumbs-down to a National Museum of Unhappiness. (2018)

Liam Kennedy:

How is it that my good friend and great man of literature, Jack Foster, can be so wrong about matters as varied as Brexit and a Museum of the Troubles? More seriously, his critique ('Why the last thing we all need is a Museum of the Troubles', Comment, February 14) is both thoughtful and heartfelt. I would commend it to all of us who inhabit the "narrow ground" that is Northern Ireland.

Jack begins, and rightly so, by questioning the euphemism "the Troubles". He prefers the "Years of Disgrace". Others have their own summary phrase. For some those years of conflict represented a continuation of the civil rights campaign of the 1960s, but pursued by other means. For others the descent into street violence at the end of the 1960s resulted from a communist-republican conspiracy. Far-fetched as both views may seem, they are lines of interpretation of the Troubles that were sincerely held.

That is what is so wonderful about history (we'll come to heritage in a moment): it offers context and perspective and seeks to present well-grounded interpretations in place of myth, half-truth and wishful thinking.

There may be a variety of interpretations, of course, depending on value judgments, but history-making is ultimately a truth-seeking activity, however approximate and incomplete the current narratives may turn out to be. And it makes space for different voices.

Thus, I would have no difficulty in representing either of the two positions above in a Museum of the Troubles, but alongside many, many other voices.

Years ago I came to the unfashionable conclusion that "the Troubles" wasn't all that bad as a label for the conflict. Here was a complicated theatre of violence involving the Army, the RUC, various republican factions and various loyalist factions. Moreover, there was intense struggle within the two major political communities as between constitutionalists and militants.

The people's phrase, the Troubles, captures the muddled and the many-sided nature of the conflict and has troubling psychological connotations.

"Museums in divided societies work only when history can be turned into heritage," my friend proclaims. I'm not sure of the basis for this grand generalisation and I note that the Americans, for one, have not delayed the opening of a National Museum of African-American History and Culture until such time as the racist residues still present in US society have been neutralised. I would suggest we have come a long way since the mayhem of the 1990s and collective amnesia will hardly help with outstanding issues. There seems to be a danger of present-mindedness here, of allowing current difficulties to obscure longer-term trends.

But, even if valid, let's confront the problem head-on, making ourselves international leaders rather than followers. Through the popular medium of a Troubles Museum, or a Troubles Complex, there is an opportunity to deepen understanding of our contested history, to confront rebarbative aspects of our recent past and also to see how ordinary men and women, speaking through the medium of oral and other archives, struggled to lead lives in the midst of killing and destruction.

Then there are the songwriters, poets, musicians, artists, satirists, photographers and filmmakers, who responded in different ways to the times in which we were trapped. There is a story of many colours to be told here, both to ourselves and to visitors from abroad.

I can understand how Jack Foster, and indeed others such as the former MLA Basil McCrea, should have concerns about how the project might deal with atrocities in the past, from that of McGurk's bar in the 1970s to Loughinisland in the 1990s. I acknowledge there is a real challenge here, with a need for sensitivity of a high order and a dialogue with victims and survivors.

In the original article (January 31) I spoke of a narrative arc – the changing times of the 1960s, the descent into violence in the 1970s and the achievements of the Good Friday Agreement and beyond. There is much more than simply bloodshed in our recent history.

It may well be that the Troubles needs to be contextualised within the longer and broader history of the north, or of Belfast, but it would be economic and financial illiteracy on the part of policy-makers not to recognise that the world beyond our shores identifies (or misidentifies) Northern Ireland with the Troubles.

What is proposed is more than a museum: it is a project that seeks to fuse economic, social and cultural objectives. Not least there is an urgent need for a means of dealing with the legacy of the past.

This could be a doorway into another time, offering possibilities of understanding and empathy. There is also the prospect of an oral history archive, of other Troubles-related archives (documents, newspapers, cartoons, memoirs, photos, film and TV footage).

Additional modules might include a Peace and Research Centre as originally mooted, but which was ploughed into the mud out at Moira, temporary exhibition spaces that addressed conflicts, peace and reconciliation processes elsewhere, the centralisation of some victim-support services, as well as linkages to other cultural and heritage centres in Belfast and beyond.

One could imagine a summer season of Troubles-related plays, poetry readings or films, thereby drawing the Lyric Theatre, the Black Box, Crescent Arts Centre or Queen's Film Theatre into a web of related experiences, catalysed initially by a visit to the Troubles Complex.

There are two further elements I'd like to bring under the spotlight.

All of us have had the experience of being questioned by visitors as to living in a divided society, of its contested histories and much else. How do people know who's a Catholic or who's a Protestant? There is no reason why there should not be an auditorium within the complex where professional tutors conduct mini-discussions on the questions that bubble upwards following the immersive experience of voyaging through the galleries. This should be particularly valuable for schoolchildren, young people and the naturally curious.

Secondly, there is the question of religion, but not in the usual sense. What separates Northern Ireland from places like Croatia, Bosnia and Serbia in the 1990s is the role played by the mainstream Churches in not espousing "faith and fatherland" stances. The Troubles was many things. It was not a jihad. The major Churches merit a place of respect within the complex and might afford a place of sanctuary for visitors finding themselves troubled by the experience.

Finally, to take up the thorny issue of politics that Jack raises, there is indeed the problem of a bagful of Kilkenny cats. Our politicians, in other words.

Still, a city that named a span across the Connswater as the Sam Thompson Bridge, a decision freighted with the symbolism of bridging difference, of trade union solidarity and of people's creativity, is capable of setting down principled guidelines and then stepping back and allowing an array of independent talents, from architects and archivists to curators, historians and computer scientists, to work on what could be another jewel in the crown of a once industrial powerhouse that is now re-emerging as a cool, but edgy, city. (2018)

1   On January 30, 2018 Professor Kennedy published an article in the *Belfast Telegraph*: "Why we need a museum of the Troubles". This was my reply which was published on February 13 as "Why the last thing we all need is a museum of the Troubles". Professor Kennedy's reply to my reply appeared on February 18 as "Critics of my plan for a museum of the Troubles are sincere, but misguided" and with the author's permission it appears below. Further correspondence ensued. (2023)

2   "But it is hard to feel anything other than dismay when it comes to the legacy of the Troubles. The first point to make is that is it not in fact correct to describe it as the legacy of the past. It is the legacy of terrorism." – *News Letter* editorial, July 18, 2023. (2023)

3   And also his essential book, *Who was Responsible for the Troubles? The Northern Ireland Conflict* (2020). (2023)

Morning in Mexico

It is morning in Mexico, on the Pacific coast hours south of Puerto Vallarta. I am on a patio in La Manzanilla shaded by hibiscus bushes with magnificent frigate-birds (magnificent in name and in appearance) floating overhead as I reach for a second cup of coffee. Fittingly, I'm reading the English writer D.H. Lawrence's *Mornings in Mexico* (1927) which combines his familiar intensity and eloquent insistence. I have not read Lawrence for years but he was an early inspiration whose restless life in sunny climes and writings in such dazzling colour were an escape from the grey provincialism of Northern Ireland that caged the upstart sparrow of a student that I then was.

I intended to write my Master of Arts thesis on Lawrence under the supervision of the late Philip Hobsbaum, the Bradford-raised poet and critic, author of *A Reader's Guide to D.H. Lawrence*. He was then an English lecturer at Queen's University, Belfast who encouraged Seamus Heaney, Michael Longley and other Ulster poets and without whom the poetry scene in Northern Ireland from the later 1960s would look very different. Like those poets, I am indebted to Hobsbaum. My supervisor like Lawrence was fearlessly outspoken, a virtue in short supply among our educated classes, especially in the matter of how our lives and our politics interact, usually to the detriment of our lives. Too often, political discussion in Northern Ireland means the exchange of predictable volleys from fixed positions.

Lawrence was a fierce individualist who detested group-think of the kind that dominates our rancid political and increasingly our cultural scene. But this morning, here in La Manzanilla, I am reflecting more on how I ever got to the privileged vantage-point of choosing at university whether or not to study the writings of D.H. Lawrence and, indeed, evading the Irish winter in the heat of Jalisco state. In the end I chose not to study Lawrence but not because our long-time family doctor in Belfast was appalled that I would be working on "that dirty writer" – the notorious *Lady Chatterley's Lover* obscenity trial was recent, so this would have been three years later.

In the beginning it was thanks to English tax-payers and successive British governments. Why not give credit where credit is due? Like Lawrence, I came from a working-class family. My mother and father left school in east Belfast at thirteen. But my father, by dint of the apprentice's exertion of going to night-school, eventually became a draughtsman in the Sirocco Works, the great engineering firm that began by making tea-machinery for India and got into ventilation and air-conditioning, making the immense fans for RMS *Titanic* and other Harland & Wolff behemoths of the sea.

In those days, night-schools who awarded the Lower and Higher National certificates were the old Mechanics Institutes and opened no highway to the humanities. This meant my father never developed his natural inclinations and toiled unhappily in an office where with sad irony he died one morning, returning home that evening at his customary hour but this time in a coffin. Working-class women for their part could hope only to be housewives, or typists and tracers in some firm in the industrial city of Belfast until they got married. My mother, like many women of the period, sublimated her intelligence and flair in various women's organizations and almost frenetic daily socializing ("colloguing", was my father's term for it).

I would not have had Lawrence's brilliance or tenacity to graduate out of the working class without the possibility of going to grammar school and then – miraculous on hindsight – to university where I was exposed to some remarkable minds. I gratefully recall Jeremy Roxbee-Cox, a shy young English lecturer (they were almost all English in those days) teaching us epistemology (the theory of knowledge) simply by conducting an argument in a seamless monologue while gazing out of the window. I was being shown how to think. Basking in the examples of the philosopher Professor W.B. Gallie, Philip Hobsbaum, the Sri Lankan lecturer in English Gamini Salgado, and the social anthropologist Rosemary Harris, I unfolded like an hibiscus flower – at least in my own imagination![1]

None of it would have happened without the English conservative politician R.A. Butler and the Education Act of 1944. I thank him and the Northern Ireland politicians who extended the Act to the province in 1947. They changed my life forever. And the lives of my generation, as well as the social and political life of Northern Ireland.

My contemporaries at Queen's included Catholic and Protestant beneficiaries of the Education Act who became leaders of the civil rights movement of the late 1960s, Catholic and Protestant, including Kevin Boyle, Erskine Holmes, Eamonn McCann and Paddy Lynch among my cohort. (As an undergraduate, in miniature emulation and contrariness, I modelled myself instead on the young James Joyce, the aloof literary student who put aesthetics above political activism.) That particular form of group-think was a liberating good under the circumstances. But understandably it pre-empted any feeling of gratitude for a free first-class education and stimulating avenue into knowledge and the life of the mind. Higher education has always been about accessing credentials, and now it is, alas, especially in English, a swerve away from the aesthetics of literature into social justice.

But I hope there is still the excitement of discovery on the campuses today. The English poet John Keats unforgettably likened his amazed discovery of the world of poetry and learning, while reading in his room, to the "wild surmise" of the conquistador

Hernan Cortez when he encountered the Pacific Ocean for the first time. That was how I felt, too, when a student at Queen's, in the library or the lecture-room.

But I had experienced the thrill of discovery even earlier, at Annadale Grammar School while being taught by the impressive D.B. Erskine (ex-World War Two tank commander) and bolting down – food for thought and feeling – the marvellous pale-green-bound *Pageant of English Verse*, edited by E.W. Parker with "Property of the Belfast Education Authority" stamped on its title page. A powerful Lawrence poem called "Snake" uncoiled from its later pages. I tip my mortar-board to the old BEA.

Unlike Keats's, my discovery eventually took me literally to the New World when I graduated from Queen's and lit out apprehensively for Oregon to pursue a PhD.. Poetry and the Pacific became one. Keats was a working-class boy, too, and didn't have a teacher to correct him in his history. It was not Cortez but the traveller Vasco Nunez de Balboa who was perhaps the first European to stand on the shore of the Pacific. (Keats's sonnet loses nothing of its magical power with this error.) Cortez was the conqueror of Mexico where I sit this morning under cloudless skies.

Keats was indebted to George Chapman, the English playwright who translated the Greek Homer. I sit in Mexico equally indebted – in the first instance to the English lawmakers who expanded the education system, and then to the teachers who tuned that system to the development of more and more young minds. Gratitude costs nothing, except, it seems, in our corner of the world where it might be misconstrued by the tribe as the wrong politics.

And there is also obligation in learning. Keats felt obliged to return the gift of his discovery back to the world as published verse. Education and identity are intimately entwined. I am Irish, certainly, but I am British, not least courtesy of my liberating free education, among other things. I simply cannot envisage life divorced from the society that enabled me to sit here in Jalisco (suddenly and happily distracted by a black and yellow Mexican cacique in the bushes), making the re-acquaintance of one of my early emancipators and role-models, the wandering Lawrence who nonetheless England made. (2018)

1 Because I had little interest then in the history of science, I didn't take a class in the School of Philosophy from John Herivel whom I often passed on University Square, and regret I didn't. Born in Belfast and educated at Methodist College, Herivel later became one of the sharpest of the wartime codebreakers at Bletchley Park and was the first to break into the Nazi cipher machine called "the Red". He afterwards taught maths at Campbell College in east Belfast (where earlier C.S. Lewis had been a pupil) and was then appointed maths lecturer at Queen's before shifting his field to the history and philosophy of science. (2023)

Bellwethers or Allweathers?

There is a story gaining traction I first read in the *Irish Times* three months ago.

A unionist businessman ("born into a unionist background"), living near the border, thought that if a few more unionists like him are convinced that Irish unification is the future, changing demographics would soon overwhelm the others. Denis Bradley's *Irish Times* article (February 21) is condescendingly entitled, "How do you solve a problem like unionism?" (despite its *Sound of Music* playfulness) and name-checks two very highly respected unionists to lend his narrative of imminent transformation its leading characters.[1] The late Dr John Robb was a notable Northern Irish surgeon who worked in the service of reconciliation between Planter and Gael. He came from a Presbyterian tradition that has an all-Ireland perspective; he was a senator in the Republic of Ireland for seven years. John Dunlop CBE (like Denis Bradley an honorary Doctor of Laws) was a Presbyterian minister in Jamaica before becoming minister of the Rosemary Street Presbyterian Church in Belfast and then Moderator of the General Assembly of the Presbyterian Church in Ireland; he has been prominent in the cause of cultural diversity in Northern Ireland. Dr Bradley quotes Dunlop from twenty years ago: "We [unionists] are a people who live behind spiritual, political and ecclesiastical ramparts". Well, unionists were certainly under constitutional siege then and still are, but I can't testify to the spiritual or ecclesiastical.   For the record, the constitutional rampart is the only one I live behind and that one surely is easily explicable: it stands between me and a united Ireland that wishes to sunder me from the UK. The Rev. Dunlop was right that too rarely does unionism take the initiative in the cause of its own flourishing.

Gary Gibbon, Channel 4's political editor, retells this same story in his blog, "Forty Shades of Green, Fifty Shades of Orange", likewise deploying the formula of the high-profile unionist thinking the unthinkable. Gibbon's first leading character is Professor Jim Dornan, "from a unionist background". Because Professor Dornan is "a world-renowned gynaecologist" now thinking of backing a united Ireland, the implication is that lesser mortals will follow suit. The more so, perhaps, because his son Jamie is a screen actor (star of *Fifty Shades of Grey*, hence the "fifty shades of orange").[2] Mr Gibbon's other leading character is Ian Marshall, former President of the Ulster Farmers' Union and now a senator in Dáil Éireann. Mr Marshall explains his change of heart thus: "Yeah, I'm a realist, I'm a pragmatist". Dornan and Marshall are meant to suggest that business and the professions are soft-hearted on the Union because they are hard-headed in everything else.

Those with skin in the game hurry the story along. "Irish unification is no longer a question of 'if', rather it is one of 'how soon'," Alban Maginness, a Social and Democratic Labour Party politician, and thus a constitutional nationalist, told readers of the *Belfast Telegraph*. In another blog, Gibbon claims that "respected figures from the liberal wing of unionism are now ready to talk with the government in Dublin about Irish unity".

But is there really talk "even amongst some DUP sources" about "shifting plates" and "creaking glaciers"? Or is this Gibbon's attempt at self-fulfilling prophecy? Presentiments of a united Ireland are a political intervention, so we should expect more of them soon.

The storytellers are surely splashing about in shallow water. Unionism and Irish unification, both tripping off the tongue, in reality involve, through time and space, the practice of governance, social mores, belief systems, value systems, understandings of citizenship. I for one am not just "of a unionist background" (as though Britishness were a replaceable stage backdrop to front-stage Irishness) – but have a UK foreground and middle-ground too. That does not prevent me from enjoying the complex weave of my Irishness, any more than it prevents those southern Irish born, living and working in the UK (for example, all those Irish correspondents of the BBC) from enjoying the weave of their undeclared Britishness. My wish is to see above all peace and harmony in Northern Ireland and all of us in the British-Irish archipelago drawing closer together.

Professor Dornan in the *Belfast Telegraph* (May 18, 2018) acknowledges the fine education, health care and "everything else" by which he has prospered in the United Kingdom, but finds them outweighable: "if somebody offers me a good deal then I would go for it". Professor Dornan's "good deal" might be a thinking unionist's bad dream. But like me and his son, Jamie's father is one of David Goodhart's "Anywheres", cushioned from political impact by moveable credentials and – though not in my own case – being well-off. Or we might call us "Allweathers": "Blow wind, come wrack", at least our choice of habitation's at our beck (modestly in my case, whereas "Jamie Dornan sells his £5 million Cotswold house but where is he moving to next?", Gloucestershirelive.co.uk, June 20, 2022). The landlocked unionist "Somewheres" (rooted in time and place in east Belfast, County Antrim and along the border and elsewhere) would have no say in a deal cooked up by republicans and the privileged ones "from a unionist background".

I can see the attraction of a wholly practical approach to citizenship. An Irish passport for easy entrance to the post-Brexit EU would be handy. But would the Irish state have welcomed my cynical attitude to Irish citizenship? I hope not. Malachi O'Doherty thinks the English who prefer poverty to being in the European Union are "bloody-minded". But this was the precise choice made by the southern Irish in 1922: they chose poverty over staying in the United

Kingdom. I admire them for it. Their poverty lasted decades. Good on them, I say. They believed their ethno-cultural identity would be honoured best in an independent country. We don't know how many of their northern descendants would make the same honourable choice, even if leaving the UK would not be "a good deal". For some of them, a border poll would be an invitation to a homecoming.

As it happened, the Free State developed in ways unacceptable to those who preferred to remain in the United Kingdom. One strand of that society was a diehard Sinn Féin party. Professor Dornan is reported as daydreaming a united Ireland in which Sinn Féin obligingly fade away like UKIP after Brexit, mission accomplished. He forgets that Sinn Féin are an all-Ireland party intent on governing the island that it will not cease to harass until it achieves its foretold consummation.

Mr O'Doherty is right to say that were a united Ireland to win a border poll, the crucial Yes voters would not be Sinn Féin supporters.[3] But is that because Sinn Féin have via Brexit cleverly mainstreamed the idea of a united Ireland and are currently letting Leo Varadkar and Simon Coveney do the heavy lifting?

The real cause of a united Ireland, Mr O'Doherty insists, would be that unionism is "about Protestantism, monarchy, social conservatism, and reverence for the British Army and imperial history". My own unionism is historically indeed about those things but also about other things too numerous to mention, involving culture (but not explicit Protestant theology) and, when necessary, liberal reform. Social conservatism has characterised immoderate unionism, but the error of confusing the essence of unionism with the practice of the DUP is unhelpful save to prompt people like me to explain their different unionism.

Unionism is originally about kinship and shared experience with the Scots, Welsh and English. That is why, by definition, my unionism could not have "a continuing identity in a united Ireland" as Mr O'Doherty encourages. Not because it is brittle or fragile, but because it is too big for a united Ireland. I would be compelled to substitute Dublin for London as my capital. I would have my unambiguous British citizenship rescinded. I would inhabit an enclave, be at best a West Brit, that once reviled status now enjoyed by the Dublin élite, but secretly.

But isn't it unfair to expect nationalists to live unself-consciously in the UK while refusing as a unionist to live in an Irish republic? Yes. But I see the UK, all told, as the preferred option because I presumptuously believe (perhaps wrongly) that many Northern Irish Catholics and moderate nationalists are less unhappy in a rapidly diversifying UK (and a more politically symmetrical NI) than unionists would be in a far less diverse and symmetrical Irish republic.

I admit that Brexit has been the catalyst in the resurgence of border-poll nationalism. But as a voter I was faced with a dilemma. To vote Leave was to create uncertainty in Ireland. To vote Remain was to remand the UK in the custody of a vast bureaucracy. I chose the former and, to me, lesser evil.

Malachi O'Doherty judges the decision to privilege UK citizenship over NI residency as offensive to moderate nationalists. That I regret, since I have always said No to any party that offended constitutional nationalists. But since I have Catholic friends who are firm Brexiteers, the judgement might be harsh. But it is an honour to cross swords with Malachi O'Doherty, our indispensable honest broker. He implies that he too faces a dilemma, like others "of a nationalist background".

It won't be resolved by pragmatic "good deals". Nor by the DUP or Sinn Féin. That leaves a joint and public exploration of the shared and unshared cultures that create the dilemmas. The impending sea-change narrative just does not ring true. (2018/2022)

1   Dr Denis Bradley, a former priest, is a freelance journalist and former vice-chairman of the Northern Ireland Policing Board. He was awarded an honorary Doctor of Laws by the University of Ulster in 2005.

2   In December 2023, Jamie (now inhabiting the borderless virtual world of popular moviemaking), told the *Radio Times*: "I'm very open-minded to the idea of a united Ireland" and, like his father, referred only to factors irrelevant to citizenship and nationality: health, education and the economy. (His distinguished father died in 2021 after contracting COVID-19.) (2023)

3   "If there ever is a united Ireland", *Belfast Telegraph*, April 22, 2018.

Your Tribe or Mine?

Amy Chua's *Political Tribes: Group Instinct and the Fate of Nations* and J.D. Vance's *Hillbilly Elegy: A Memoir of a Family and Culture in Crisis* have a special cousinage, which I will disclose later. In the meantime, enough to say that J.D. Vance's book is a case-study in Amy Chua's interpretation of the United States today and, by ambitious generalisations, of the rest of the world, not just today but always.

The uncertain American present, though, is Chua's immediate concern. She sees the United States at a cross-roads, demographically, politically and socially, and the cross-roads by definition enforces division. White Americans are about to become a minority in "their own" country and Trump's election to the presidency is a reflection of the baffled anxieties and acute resentments that this is generating. Chua knows, of course, that ethnic disturbance has always been a feature of American life; but up to now the tension between binding American patriotism and centrifugal group competitiveness has been held to a reasonable and productive equitability, and the profitable and efficient functioning of the country has not been in doubt. This is changing and the United States is historically ill-equipped to manage, or even understand, the process of cultural, social and political tribalism, or dissociation, that is accelerating in the nation.

Ironically, the apparent domestic success of American democracy and the powerful myth of the melting-pot are the source of the ill-equipment. The democracy shipped abroad has been a monolithic one, the broadest of careless brushstrokes inspired by free-market capitalism and a belief in unfettered individualism. Chua provides four extended case-studies in recent American foreign involvement (chiefly military) – Vietnam, Iraq, Afghanistan and Venezuela. These illustrate the limitations of American democracy in managing or ruling other societies and the foolish belief in American society's exportability. They also illustrate the ruinous counter-productivity of imposed democratic rule, the unleashing of anti-democratic factionalism (one might also add corruption) that democracy paradoxically enables. And when she says tribalism, Chua means it: she tells us that Afghanistan's "national" anthem mentions fourteen ethnic groups.

Chua contrasts these disastrous American interventions and withdrawals with the ability of 40,000 British soldiers and bureaucrats to govern 200 million Indians for two centuries, a "success" made possible precisely by British education into the factions and "tribes" that might in British ignorance have early subverted the Raj. Chua does not say so, but out of this local study and knowledge during the Empire came the British discipline of social anthropology.

Hence America's frustrated confronting of what is happening inside its own borders. There, too, individualism, free-market capitalism and American parliamentary democracy are newly at serious odds with proliferating groups (ethnic, sexual, religious, regional) exercising energetic lobbying power and threatening both the implicit and vaunted unanimity of the American Dream. The long-term haunting question is whether some of them portend the ethno-nationalist divisiveness that the United States and Europe witnessed, for example, in post-Tito, democratised Yugoslavia. The United States as a "super-group" that claims the fidelity of its distinctive components is in danger of failing.

For Chua it is more than an American problem, witness her reference to France's struggle to maintain *laïcité* in the (veiled) face of Islam. And to England's laissez-faire response as Muslim enclaves develop in the cities and towns, a case of the old imperial wisdom vanished or inappropriate on the home front, the will to govern embarrassed by the discrediting of Empire. Or simply English and other European societies being overwhelmed by a global force their leaders do not comprehend. Indeed, Chua sees professed Enlightenment values and principles – liberalism, secularism, rationality, equality, free marketry – not only in process of being challenged at home by a much older and often inadvertently imported tribalism but actually provoking into activity its tribal enemies.

It is a co-dependent dynamic. A gulf is widening between, on the one hand, the metropolitan liberal elites (David Goodhart's "Anywheres", we might remind Chua), who are their own tribe, according to Chua, innocent believers in universalism and not so innocent believers in the global economy, and, on the other hand, the hinterland (Goodhart's rooted, stationary but increasingly restive "Somewheres"; the Empire at home, as it were). Trump has been the beneficiary of the "Empire" striking back, a phenomenon facilitated by the reduction of small town and country white Americans, poor or of modest means, to an aggrieved faction or tribe in "their own" country in which they used to participate as the ruling majority.

If globalism is one provocation to inherent tribal impulses, another is, to use Chua's own 2003 coinage, market-dominant minorities. She recounts the age-old resentment in Vietnam to Chinese commercial dominance (something which to their cost the American occupiers either did not know or care about), and tells us something I was not aware of: that most of the Vietnamese Boat People in the first wave of flight were in fact ousted minority Chinese. Today, the 3% Chinese population of Indonesia controls up to 70% of the private economy; in the Philippines, 2% controls the corporate, banking, airline, shipping and retail sectors.

Are British Columbians aware of this? Since around 2008 when I left Vancouver, the metropolis has undergone a sea-change brought about by the overnight installation of an economic Chinese elite encouraged by greedy municipal, provincial and federal governments, with the result that private property (the cornerstone of Chinese investment culture) is beyond the financial reach of British Columbians helpless to meet the competition from innumerable mainland Chinese billionaires. Whole neighbourhoods have had their social fabric unravelled beyond repair. The government retreat has belatedly started and the backlash begun among those who now are forced to perceive themselves as a comparatively impoverished and increasingly unhoused population in "their own" country. What was missing from the get-go was any Euro-Canadian knowledge of the dynamics of recent Chinese culture (or of any culture, for that matter): Canadians knew only the old quietist, colourful but static, nationalist Chinese culture that inhabited Chinatown; the old imperial wisdom once again gone missing until a British-born BC geographer, David Ley, recently brought that culture to light in the austere pages of the *International Journal of Housing Policy.*

But mention of British Columbia is a reminder that even knowledge of Chinese economic intentions would have been inadequate in the face of a force that oddly Chua soft-shoes around, lending her study a curious sense of cultural passivity: her book is full of those to whom things are happening or who are ignorant of what they are doing; it is scantily peopled by agents and policymakers. Like most Americans, Chua pays small attention to her northern neighbour. Canada's pioneering Multiculturalism was a deliberate policy that created a self-conscious ethnic plurality across the Canadian vastness through language and cultural impositions. These ethno-cultural autonomies have been encouraged to grow and surely fit Chua's definition of tribalism, with similar developments in the process of Multiculturalism occurring in New Zealand and Australia.[1]

Multiculturalism imposes certain harsh sanctions. Among them are the costs in reputation and damaging political attribution of motive of anyone who attempts to identify ethnicity except in an exclusively positive light. This meant that what quickly became an acute social problem in Vancouver when offshore Chinese money avalanched in could not be identified, and therefore solved, because the ethno-cultural source of the sudden and deep real-estate investments, often by absentee investors, could not be spoken of. A few Vancouver journalists bravely followed Ley in spilling the beans.

The United States does not have a government Multicultural programme and policy and relies instead on the rather debased coinage of a unifying American Dream. But unofficially, as in western Europe, Multiculturalism, though not quite the state religion it virtually is in Canada ("Diversity is our strength," Justin Trudeau chants at every opportunity), encourages, indeed sanctions, Chua's tribalism and the by now firmly ensconced identity politics and political correctness that ensue from it. The process of diversification, dissociation and proliferation that Chua laments is hardly to be wondered at. Even back in 1983 when I became a Canadian citizen, I was told by the Citizenship Commissioner that I was not required to give up anything of my existing culture. Coming from Northern Ireland, I knew this to be foolish counsel.

Chua descants on one of the accompaniments of identity politics: the battle of cultural appropriation. She gives recent American examples (including the hostility directed at Beyoncé's traditional Indian bridal outfit) but this is old Canadian hat (long before the Mexican sombreros that drew the ire of those thirsting for offence at the University of East Anglia in 2015). Twenty-five years ago the Director of the Canada Council proposed that no literary or artistic project be funded that depicted a culture (read "ethnic group" or "female gender") *of which the applicant was not himself a member*. On the heels of a report from its Advisory Committee for Racial Equality in the Arts, the Council decided that "cultural appropriation is a serious issue". To the great credit of the novelist Timothy Findley ("Stop. Now.") and other Canadian writers, including Neil Bissoondath ("I reject the idea of cultural appropriation completely"), the idea was murdered in its cradle before it matured into a fiat. It would have introduced the idea of apartheid (or tribalism) of the creative imagination which itself might have seemed to the government employees of the Canada Council like a logical extension of the policy of Multiculturalism. Retaining as property your own gender and ethnic experiences and imaginings, and having them subsidised and protected by the government, might have seemed no different from retaining your own subsidised language and customs while living in Canada. (Female genital mutilation and Sharia Law have been a bit of a problem in that regard.) But as we now know, the transgression of cultural appropriation has recently been put back on the books, as it were, in the United States and Britain and in Canada itself.

Chua defines tribes as groups with vested interests that compose a political or quasi-political agenda. That agenda has increasingly taken the form of collective grievance, the claim that the group is being wronged, even oppressed and that redress must be total and immediate lest there be protest and agitation. Multiculturalism has, of course, by rooting itself in the notion that distinctive group identities must be preserved, encouraged not only perpetual collective vigilance but also the active *formation* of groups that did not previously exist, such as the numerous (and activist) genders now officially recognised in Canada and elsewhere. And among those groups there is a hotly contested *hierarchy* of victimhood and rights deprivation.

Tribalism and ethnic diversity are ancient realities, which nationalism can both encourage and protect against. (Justin Trudeau manages to believe that lack of a definable nationality in the ordinary sense defines Canada as a nation.) London has long been renowned for its ethnic diversity, but it is both *the scale* and *the speed* of change that in London and elsewhere in the West have caught us unawares. In Ben Judah's remarkable *This is London: Life and Death in the World City* (2016) – a book Chua should have read – ethnic diversity is displayed in truly intimate detail. But the capital city that is now

55% non-white British is not the diverse city we thought we knew; it seems in Judah's depiction more like George Orwell's Wigan made vast, or even Conrad's London at the opening of *Heart of Darkness* somehow fast-forwarded to the 21st century. Read Judah and you will never see Soho quite the same way again.

The problem Chua is trying to explain and solve is one of acute recent juxtapositions, of sudden changing power roles among groups, of emerging wide-ranging political ramifications. At the back of it all, perhaps, is the decline in dominance of white western Euro-Americans who devised and encouraged the very diversification that now threatens their power and who are yet the sole villain of the Multicultural piece. Douglas Murray in *The Strange Death of Europe* (2017) has written of a curious and possibly fatal European failure of will in the matter. For the white, London-Scottish Murray to deplore the cultural fall-out from Multiculturalism and European immigration policy is a perilous undertaking whereas as an American whose Chinese parents immigrated from the Philippines, Chua is licensed to speak in such broad ethnic and racial terms. Multiculturalism has encouraged the rollback from free expression and frank discussion, substituting instead carefully monitored speech in which the identity of the speaker, not the truth-value of what is said, is paramount: candid observation and opinion rarely now stimulate debate but often instead provoke fury and grotesquely exaggerated reaction. Chua's candour is nevertheless welcome and helpful.

It was a surprise to come upon Chua's name towards the end of J.D. Vance's *Hillbilly Elegy*. That in this rags-to-academic riches life-story Chua is Vance's law professor at Yale explains the fulsome endorsement of *Political Tribes* on the hardback's front cover and Chua's equally fulsome endorsement of that life-story before the reader has reached the Contents page. And indeed, Vance's life before education rescued him was one of Chua's cases in point. *Hillbilly Elegy* is a very good read (if its virtues are overblown that is because of its refreshing candour) and an almost alarming diptych of both

Kentucky "Somewheres" doomed to be mired in their own static Appalachian culture unless they find the strength to become luckless inhabitants of the post-industrial Rust Belt to the north (Vance's early life was lived between the Kentucky hills and small-town Ohio – between the frying pan and the fire) who voted for Trump *en masse*.[2]

Oddly, Vance's intriguing misery-memoir loses momentum when it reverses itself and he reaches Yale; a certain self-satisfaction sets in as Chuck Berry's·poor boy, as it were, gets on the line to us from the Promised Land. Yale, of course, is one of Chua's own tribes and Vance bored me a little with its tribal characteristics, though I realise he is trying to reveal the difficult rites that must be performed before full membership can be gained. It is his hillbilly upbringing, introduced by his initial modesty, that is the real attraction of the book, and the account of his own early travails is fascinating and peopled with family figures larger than life, Mamaw and Papaw among them.

Still, one important piece of the bigger picture he is trying to draw for us is sloppily inserted. His premiss, personal and political, is that he identifies with, and is a spokesman for, the deprived "millions of working-class white Americans of Scots-Irish descent". Unfortunately, he displays no interest whatsoever in the origin or dynamics of the Scots-Irish race. One wonders if he even knows the etymology of "hillbilly" – "billy boys", followers of King Billy (King William III), Ulster Protestants who settled in their thousands in the Appalachians in the eighteenth century but also roved along the frontier which they took a firm hand in extending. Vance simply means white working-class Americans. His social anthropology is as lax as his professor's when she uses tribe to mean simply a self-asserting group, a possibly insensitive use of "tribe" in the United States for which Multiculturalism gives her license. Since my parents and grandparents grew up in working-class Protestant east Belfast, I too am of the Scots-Irish. The traits of the real Scots-Irish – including a gift for being their own worst enemy – came across the

Atlantic with them. Their achievement in the early days speaks to their virtues and advantages – their anti-authoritarianism and hard-working self-dependence. However, they were also suspicious, confrontational, self-centred and parochial (despite their wanderlust), begrudging, sceptical and pessimistic. Under normal circumstances, never easy people to help as perhaps mid-West America and Northern Ireland today are proving.

The apparent slightness of Vance's historical knowledge of the Scots-Irish, and his absorption of them into blue-collar America is, however, telling. The successful Scots-Irish of the 18th and early 19th centuries vanished into the mainstream of successful America they helped create and govern and now their poorer cousins are once again mainstreamed, this time disadvantageously. Either way, they lost the honorific ethnic identity that Catholic Irish-Americans have enjoyed and resolutely maintained, helped by the history of the urban enclaves they formed. Some see the fate of the Scots-Irish back in Northern Ireland as precarious, politically and culturally. If so, it is Chua's study that might explain some of the dynamics involved in current Northern Irish society. I'm not alluding to the sectarian component of Sinn Féin or to the IRA as, in Chua's terms, an ethno-nationalist terror-group, though these are part of the historical background. I allude instead to how – in Chua's formulation – increasing "democratization" has encouraged ethno-nationalism.

By democratization I mean the greater, more widespread, voluntary and vocal civic participation in Northern Ireland by Catholics, a greater interest in the laws, customs and value-systems of the country. The situation was very different in the 1920s through the 1950s when the Catholic populace was a resentful minority with an abstentionist mindset in face of a sectarian unionism and with relatively few educated champions. The 1960s, when young people began to reap the benefit of the 1947 Education Act, saw rudimentary versions of Vance's own escape via higher education from the mental and physical laager. There is now a consolidated educated and articulate Catholic professional class that was emerging during, and helping to orchestrate, the civil rights movement.

To the extent that that movement was a facet of a larger Irish nationalist dissatisfaction, there has been a continuity between now and then, a continuity that for a few decades was like an underground cable and has now resurfaced. Liberal unionists hoped that greater Catholic participation in the life of Northern Ireland meant that Northern Ireland was emerging as one of Chua's "super-groups" in which the disparate ethnic and cultural components pledge allegiance to the higher entity. For a few years this century this seemed achievable but suddenly the hope has suffered a reversal, triggered but not caused by Brexit. True, there is in the professional class I refer to the appearance of global urban liberalism. Members attach much importance to "rights" (especially "human rights") and give the impression of wishing to see all the "tribes" (in Chua's sense) in Northern Ireland composing an equal mosaic.

Hope, then, for Northern Ireland? Alas, it seems not. It is odd to refer to a Catholic professional class when the Catholic church has declined so markedly. In Quebec, the Quiet Revolution of the 1960s, which saw a steep fall in the power of the Church and a growth in prosperity, resulted unexpectedly in a new confident nationalism that alarmed Trudeau, the Quebecois Scots-French Canadian federalist. So we need in Northern Ireland absolutely to distinguish "Catholic" from "nationalist", especially since there are Church-attending Catholics who are unionists though they would baulk at the name. (The distinction is hard to enact, alas, since it would be uncomfortable for a Northern Catholic of any standing to promote membership of the United Kingdom.) The spokespeople of the new Catholic professional class are in fact primarily nationalists and intend to pose an existential threat to Northern Ireland in the wake of Brexit. And as they and Sinn Féin turn their sights on the most elementary symptoms of Britishness – loyalist and Orange Order customs and insignia – loyalists in current depiction resemble Vance's displaced hillbillies in Ohio: both living shrunken post-industrial lives, both reviled and condescended to, both regarded as impediments when they were once vital assets, both becoming detached from the mainstream, islanded in their own putative bigotry. The result is an example of what has been called reverse asymmetry.

In both arenas, loyalism and Northern Ireland itself, the threat is voiced in the smooth language of Chua's cosmopolitan or Vance's campus elites, as though what exercises them is the absence of human rights across the board of Northern Ireland's population. But the recent letter signed by 200 "leading" (i.e. professional, academic and high-achieving) nationalists and addressed to the Taoiseach, Leo Varadkar, couched in the language of the *Guardian*, a letter reading as though sent from exile and bondage in the desert, could adduce only one genuine deprivation suffered by nationalists, and that is the right to live in a united Ireland entirely separated from the United Kingdom. The under-determination of the allegation of rights violation and the fact that seemingly no unionist was asked to sign the letter, suggested that underneath the cosmopolitan elitism is the old irredentist nationalism. Because it was the leader of Sinn Féin who was recorded off-camera admitting that the drive for equality would be the Trojan horse for Irish unification, that strategy was assumed to be only that of a familiar, traditional working-class republicanism.

Chua reminds us that second and third generation, British-educated Muslims in Great Britain seem to be more religious and more alienated from British society than first-generation immigrants. This suggests something like a cultural recessive gene at work, whereby tribalism is a generational as well as geographic phenomenon. But it is certainly a reminder that old strong cultures may feel no need or desire to assimilate, something that mild welcoming Canada may be learning through the troubles of Indo-Canadian society in metropolitan Vancouver.[3] The growing cultural autonomy of recent affluent Chinese immigrants (several hundred thousand) in Vancouver and Richmond, by which many of them need not speak English to lead productive lives, has been peaceful;

they are rather cut off from their Anglophone neighbours, while increasingly immigrant Greater Vancouver is itself increasingly detached from its rural hinterland. A recent internal government report on the subject has signalled alarm. But nothing will be done while the philosophy and policy of Multiculturalism are regarded as the solution to the problem they themselves created.

Against the run of play, Chua ends her book with an upbeat Epilogue. One has the impression that, unlike Scots-Irish Vance with his inherited pessimism, Chua, riding academically high and "best-selling" (she wrote *Battle Hymn of the Tiger Mother*), does not have the temperament to be depressed by her own findings; she speaks of her "congenital optimism". (Besides, best-sellers are rarely downers.) She believes that the United States will rediscover an identity adequate to its destiny as the unique super-group, once again uniting all its diverse children. I wonder. Her concluding evidence? The "blockbuster Broadway hit play *Hamilton*" in which the Founding Fathers are portrayed by black actors. The local equivalent of this very American final flourish would be to claim that *TitanicDance*, the "hit show" that is really and brazenly *LaganRiverdance* in cloth caps, is a sign that the united Ireland super-group is likely. If Northern Ireland cannot become a super-group, I cannot see the thirty-two counties becoming the viable alternative any time soon. But who knows how the Ulster Protestant "Anywheres" could jump if only the loyalists (working-class unionists) can be corralled and reduced to the impotent rump of Vance's hillbillies? (My own faint hope is that Brexit will reveal the intimacies between Ireland and Britain and offer the glimmerings of an emerging super-group of our two islands.) Northern Ireland as much as the United States is at a cross-roads, but being Scots-Irish, I don't have Chua's congenital optimism. (2018)

1   The Canadian national projects of Decolonisation and Indigenisation
    generated by the Truth and Reconciliation Commission of 2015 have
    further splintered Canadian society, the former now dismantling vestiges
    of the European, more especially British mainstream culture that gave the
    country most of its difference from its southern neighbour, the latter
    empowering and giving voice (not before time) to the Indigenous people,
    a previous subculture now being raised to cultural prominence. (2023)

2   *Hillbilly Elegy* was made into a Hollywood movie in 2020, directed by
    Ron Howard and starring Glenn Close. In 2023, Vance, a member of the
    Republican party, was elected the junior U.S. senator from Ohio. (2023)

3   Where the tensions between Sikhs and Hindus that have risen are the
    diasporic counterparts of tensions back in the subcontinent. These
    erupted into the Diwali violence in Ontario in November 2023. To this
    was added the public protests across the country on both sides of the
    Israeli-Palestinian conflict in the wake of the Hamas massacre of Israelis
    on October 7, 2023. (2023)

Two Solitudes and the Good Friday Agreement

In the many months since our devolved government evacuated Stormont, the Good Friday Agreement (GFA) of 1998 has receded from the forefront of our attention with surprising and disturbing speed.[1] It seems almost to belong to another era: events have simplified, accelerated, transmuted, and overtaken both 1998 and even 2017 when Stormont last came to a halt. From our recent and radically altered perspective, the Agreement now seems like an extraordinary Swiss-watch-like mechanism, as though an analogue solution to what has since become a digital problem.

Perhaps the Agreement's problem arose because the ingenious intricacy of the checks-and-balance mechanism was not equal to the contra-simplification of subsequent events. It was invented by committee, as it were, with the best of intentions, and meant to cover many political eventualities and shades of opinion. Moreover, the GFA presumed a coalition of the *sincerely* willing; the liberal unionist Ulster Unionist Party (UUP) and the constitutional nationalist Social Democratic and Labour Party (SDLP) were the ideal partners across the political divide. But over the years, especially after the death of Ian Paisley, whose outlandish personality ironically held it all together after the Democratic Unionist Party eclipsed the UUP, the reality degenerated into a coalition of the increasingly *un*willing.

By dint of amiable personality Martin McGuinness, late of the IRA, at first played his new role winningly and for a few years we thought that at last we had come into harbour, albeit in a ship whose dazzle livery distracted us from the point of that livery: the war that hadn't gone away, you know. For a few heady years it seemed as if the cooperation sponsored by the GFA might even strengthen a Northern Irish identity that would satisfy both political and cultural traditions. In any case, McGuinness for whatever reason decided to scuttle the ship, which was listing badly in any case and not wholly due to him and his party. By doing so (and to mix metaphors), McGuinness let something out of the bottle that might be hard to get back in.

Sinn Féin (who eclipsed the SDLP) and the DUP had become forcibly conjoined twins seeking their diametrically opposed ways of life and something eventually had to give. Increasingly, policies and events became pretexts for advancing the long-haul project (Sinn Féin's core objective of a united Ireland) or obstructing that project and protecting Northern Ireland's place in the Union (DUP). Effective day-to-day governance presumes a constitutional status quo (the GFA as an agreed terminus for the foreseeable future) and cannot proceed when endlessly motivated by thoughts of tomorrow (the GFA as a staging-post to the unification of the island).

The evacuation of Stormont has, of course, left a terrible vacuum. There is no alternative to the GFA on the near horizon: not direct rule from Westminster, not a united Ireland (despite the giddy talk of such), not Northern Ireland independence, not the simple majority rule of the rest of the United Kingdom. It is as if we are between dispensations and know only what the past one consisted of. We are now at sea, a Lilliputian local version of the dangerous between-times that W.B. Yeats recorded in "The Second Coming" (1919), though in his customary excited reverie.

Lilliputian, but still a version. The Northern Ireland Civil Rights campaign of 1968–69 was motivated by local grievances but given impetus by the Zeitgeist, by events in Paris and on American campuses, before forcibly morphing into a continuation of the Easter rebellion's unfinished business. During the Stormont hiatus (to use an optimistic word), republicans are agitating for a border poll. To them, compared to the prospect of a united Ireland, a return to Stormont, at least at the present moment, must seem to them small beer. The real trigger has been Brexit, of course. Yet even Brexit is both honouring as well as fuelling the Zeitgeist since it is part of a European convulsion that encompasses more than the United Kingdom's vote to leave the European Union. And the influence of a volatile Zeitgeist makes it more difficult to bring more immediate and proximate concerns into focus, distracting stake-holders with the lure of bigger game. Can the regional problem of Northern Ireland be solved in isolation when the big world beyond it is itself riven on such a large scale?[2]

There is a restiveness in Northern Ireland, in the UK, in the United States, in Europe. And vast though the western world is, this restlessness is larger than the sum of specific discontents and grievances, which involve mass immigration, multiculturalism, the spread of Islam, the sudden seeming instability or inadequacy of democracy. There is a drunkenness of things being various, to quote Louis MacNeice. I recall a phrase from C.P. Snow's 1954 novel, *The New Men*, set during World War Two: "events too big for men". It seems an apt recall, for there is a sense of things in the West being out of control: dispensations ending and only the ominously slouching outline of the new.

Under these influences, the two "communities" in Northern Ireland, the unionist and the nationalist, have polarised politically in an almost literal sense: each side magnetically drawn back to its pole of origin and aspiration.[3] The UUP and SDLP are in the long grass. Against the grain of history, Irish nationalism and Irish republicanism are converging. Unmoored from the interlocking obligations of the GFA, the two sides in Ulster have drifted even farther apart, the law of the excluded middle becoming more draconian. This is not, yet, thankfully, a social polarisation among the middle classes but that could still come if the political pathology metastasises. We are in danger of becoming two solitudes, at least as political collectives, though I do hope not as friends, neighbours and workmates.

Two Solitudes. Hugh Maclennan published his novel of that title in 1945, and through his main characters he tracked relations in Quebec between the majority French-Canadians on the one hand and on the other hand the English-Canadians, a ruling minority in Quebec but a ruling majority in Canada as a whole, and both founding cultures of the nation. The historical homology with Ireland, especially the north of Ireland, is for the most part striking. The problem of Two Solitudes essentially arose at roughly the same time in each country: the early 17th century. In *Two Solitudes*, Maclennan's Quebecois are Catholic, rural and agricultural, nationalistic, conservative, and determinedly French-speaking; his English-speaking Quebeckers are urban, progressive, industrialised and capitalist. The foreground denouement of the saga, with its modicum of optimism, is also familiar: what we call a mixed marriage (called that even in the novel) between the Quebecois youth (French father though Irish mother) and English-Canadian girl, though both are preceded by parents or grandparents who have in a sense courageously, and alone, crossed the sectarian divide.

Two Solitudes is set across three generations from the Great War to the onset of the Second World War. Maclennan closes his novel with the hope that the war will bring the two sides together, somehow dissolving "the two race-legends ... remembering their ancient enmities". Maclennan imagined that the country Canada was about to know itself for the first time, becoming a "super-group" in Amy Chua's recent formulation in her book *Political Tribes* (2018) when she talks about national entities that can claim the allegiance of opposing tribes. It didn't happen. The dreary tribal steeples of both Quebec and Fermanagh survived the war; indeed, the Second

World War drove a wedge between the two Irelands and conscription was a bone of contention in both provinces, Quebec and Northern Ireland.

Yet in an historical unfolding we might do well to take note of, the Quiet Revolution of the 1960s saw a sharp decline in the power of the Roman Catholic Church in Quebec which was followed by (and perhaps in part released) a surge in Quebec nationalism. Despite the previous intimacy between Catholicism and nationalism, the latter had a clearer run when its intimate was out of the picture. The nationalist surge compelled the two border polls (sovereignty referenda) in 1980 (in which independence was rejected by 59.5% of the voters) and 1995 (rejected by 50.5%). The campaigns and the years between were divisive and disturbing. There was no "Quebec City Agreement" or "Bon Vendredi Accord" to conjoin the two solitudes. Instead, the problem was solved by an epic of social engineering that dissolved one of the two Solitudes, freeing the remaining Solitude from fear. It was devised by Pierre Elliott Trudeau, Quebecois-Scots father of the current Canadian prime minister and called multiculturalism.

Likewise, the decline of the Catholic church in Ireland has not weakened nationalism, though Catholicism was long thought to be with the Gaelic language an essential girder of Irish nationalism. Once upon a time, Home Rule did indeed mean Rome Rule; time proved the Ulster Protestants absolutely right when they asserted that and nowhere have I seen it acknowledged by the Irish who themselves belatedly rebelled against the Church in the 1990s and who might have at least quietly apologised for calling northerners mere bigots when they correctly predicted the future. But the Church is no longer an argument against unification. Yet if anything, Irish republicanism has strengthened, clarified and become more assertive and sophisticated, no longer held back by what has proved to be a wounded church; indeed, able to promote itself as a reasonable, progressive, secular force. The aim, however, remains the same: imminent unification of the island.

Trudeau's remedy to end the Two Solitudes was to impose multiculturalism on the Rest of Canada (RoC) while permitting Quebec to opt out of the policy and impositions of multiculturalism and to retain control of its immigration. Responding to my deep reservations about multiculturalism in a 1993 university conference paper in Belfast in which I predicted "A Hundred Solitudes" in place of Two, a Quebec legate came up to me and told me that Quebec would never accept multiculturalism and so it has proved. The province replaced the Canadian bilingualism legislation of 1969 with the Quebec Official Language Act of 1974, reinforcing official French unilingualism with the Charter of the French Language of 1977. Quebec sovereignty aspirations have indeed subsided as Trudeau wished, but that is because Quebec is allowed to conduct itself in several vital respects like an independent country and today is quietly de-Anglicising in a manner than would have warmed the cockles of Douglas Hyde's heart in 1892. In other words, the solution to the problem of the Two Solitudes was in the dissolution of one of them, not a marriage or fusion. Meanwhile, Quebec nationalism is intent on maintaining its own Solitude whatever happens in the RoC, banking on the French language instead of the Catholic religion to deepen the solitude. And what has happened in the RoC has been the emergence of multiple solitudes through mass immigration and the generation of cultural and ethnic enclaves.

The Republic of Ireland has managed thus far, unlike Quebec, to combine a sincere desire (at least at government level) to become a multicultural society (through immigration and EU membership) with no lessening of patriotism or the nationalist desire for completion of the republican project, a 32-county independent state, that is identical to its 1916 and 1922 selves except in so far as that state would be an EU member. (Whether in the eventuality of a 32-county republic Ireland would be as dutiful a subscriber to the EU doctrine of ever-closer union, or indeed, a subscriber to multiculturalism is a moot point; might it not instead go the way of Hungary or Poland?)[4]

But multiculturalism (a largely improvised affair in Ireland unlike the prioritised and focused Canadian policy) is no more an answer to Irish unity as we imagine it today (unionists and nationalists reconciling in an Irish republic) than it is to Canadian unity (French and Anglo-Canadians interwined and intertwining with other ethnicities). Northern Irish Protestants, who for their part regard themselves as a "founding" culture, do not come in under the umbrella of Irish multiculturalism (as studies on multiculturalism in the Republic will demonstrate), any more than the Quebecois come in under the umbrella of Canadian multiculturalism. Neither group is sincerely invited to and neither wishes to. The lesson from Quebecois nationalism for Irish nationalism is that Northern Ireland must have its identity diffused through multiculturalism and immigration; Irish as an official language in Northern Ireland would advance immeasurably the republican project, and both strategies would loosen Northern Ireland's cultural and constitutional ties with the rest of the United Kingdom, just as multiculturalism has loosened Canada's cultural ties with the UK and Commonwealth, and eclipsed its own history as a senior dominion of the British Empire. Through it all, Irish like Quebec nationalism will persevere. They are not for turning.

That one can think like this is evidence of the flux at work in western societies. There is an impatience that generates scenarios and wishes to see them reach development quickly. The Good Friday Agreement by contrast was a painstakingly constructed bulwark or bridge combining enough resilience, it seemed, to absorb contingencies and with an intensely local applicability. But we may be beyond the local and merely contingent now. I believe the GFA's restoration to full working order and in sincerity on the part of the main parties is an outside chance, at least in the current swirl of politics inside and outside Northern Ireland. The new tribalism that Amy Chua identifies in the United States is old tribalism here and is if anything recently refreshed. (I recall that Seamus Heaney once remarked that the world was becoming Ulsterised.) Also, it may be that a disaffection with a government structure that compels the coalition of enemies and does not provide for the genuine opposition of parliamentary politics is too great to reverse.

What is required for the GFA to be restored is not the undignified triumphalism of the demographic contest (we witness it, aghast, during Brexit), now played with vim by some northern nationalists, but something, alas, quite alien to the current political climate.

At present, that something has no voice and has not had a voice for a long time. We suffer here the tyranny of a threadbare political discourse which dominates the public sphere and drowns out other discourses. Certainly we have a fine literature, but between it and the banal discourse of our politics there is a vacant middle. We need the literary discourse of the individual: the discourse of memoir, diary, letter that interrupts the "smelly little orthodoxies" George Orwell referred to at the end of his wonderful essay on Charles Dickens. Moreover, we need not only candid conversations between acquaintances from opposite sides of the divide ("whatever you say, say nothing" can be shackling as well as prudent advice) but to have those multiple conversations eventually rise to the surface of our public and social life, to end our enactment of the Two Solitudes. E.M. Forster's "Only connect" might be a sovereign remedy applicable not only to the uneasy silences between strangers and even friends on the constitutional predicament but also to the disconnect between, on the one hand, individual opinions and feelings about Northern Ireland's past, present and future and, on the other, the tired elementary political choices they are offered.

This is a version of a gulf between the private and public, and in Northern Ireland we have often been afraid to say in public what we really feel or think; it is often fear of our own tribe. This is an Irish form of political correctness whereby you cannot say publicly what you are thinking or feeling rather than saying in public what you are *not* thinking or feeling. There are Northern Irish Catholics (perhaps many) who are happy enough in the UK but cannot say so because of a tribal injunction. (Then there are all those Irish correspondents and presenters working for the BBC and living in England who have no public opinion on English-Irish relations because the tribal injunction crosses the water.) There are middle-class and professional unionists who can contemplate a united Ireland and some have said so, because the tribal injunction on their side is rather weaker. There are many more middle-class and professional unionists who cannot admit their unionism out of misplaced fear of being identified with tribal loyalists (though clearly many of them vote DUP). All in all, an unhealthy repression that aids the hegemony of political fundamentalism and sponsors the Two Solitudes.

The GFA tried in its own way to complicate in a mature way an otherwise simplistic political picture but did so through a complexity of political machinery and left untouched the moral maturity we also need. Orwell said that in every attack Dickens makes upon society "he is always pointing to a change of spirit rather than a change of structure"; "it is useless to change institutions without a 'change of heart'." Thinking at first that Dickens's opinion is a conservative opinion, Orwell came to see that it carries its own revolutionary potential. The Good Friday Agreement was a radical change of structure but if at the time there was a radical change of heart, an essential moral repositioning on the part of the chief participants, it has since reversed itself. Indeed, if anything the morality of our society, of our polity, of our interpretations of the past and actions in the present, has shrivelled even more since then. A change of heart requires the exercise of empathy (feeling as well as seeing the other's experience and point of view – the source of Dickens's mastery), something in short supply where we live. In the past forty-odd years I have seen what Orwell called the "native decency of the common man" stifled amidst the aridities of power politics, not only in Northern Ireland but in the UK generally, but in Northern Ireland also as the legacy of a terror campaign now retrospectively justified by its perpetrators. This justification is what Orwell called antinomianism, a blind belief in faith, a disbelief in moral and social norms.

The Good Friday Agreement was a remarkable machine, motivated in its planning and development by a behavourist notion of stimulus and reward. This was a rather patronising approach by the convenors but then obstinate and dogmatic politicians were involved. As things stand, the GFA might be reactivated but unless there is a change of heart in Orwell's sense, it will fail again and Arthur Koestler's ghost in the machine will reassert itself. I fully believe that only when Northern Ireland is through honest effort made to work can there be an agreed avenue to possible constitutional change (and who knows, perhaps a united Ireland). The innate but inadequately voiced moderateness of the majority of the Northern Irish should be the exploited motive to this end. The strands of the Agreement offer that avenue.

Monumentally, in an act of maturity, Sinn Féin must publicly postpone their destabilising call for an imminent united Ireland in favour of minding the store in which they find themselves, the here and now. If you like, they need to declare a ceasefire in their brittle demand for the endgame which lies outside the evolutionary spirit of the GFA. Otherwise, they are extending the lifetime of the Two Solitudes and the social as well as political stuntedness they maintain. (2018)

1   The Northern Ireland Assembly election was held on March 2, 2017 as a result of the resignation of the Deputy First Minister Martin McGuinness (Sinn Féin) in ostensible protest over the Renewable Heat Incentive Scandal (Ash for Cash, as it was dubbed). Sinn Féin thus collapsed the devolved government and they stayed away for three years and returned only after demanding an Irish Language Act; this was duly promised by Westminster and the Northern Irish government staggered to its feet.

2   See my essays in this book: "Your Tribe or Mine?" and "Pretendians", and my review essay, "Morbid Symptoms", on Douglas Murray's book, *The Madness of Crowds: Gender, Race and Identity* (2019) in the *Dublin Review of Books* (December 2019). Since the aftermath of George Floyd's death and the Hamas massacre of Israelis on October 7, 2023, Yeats's "The Second Coming" seems relevant on a fullscale, not Lilliputian scale.

3   The big world has further divided the two traditions in Northern Ireland, most recently and notably by way of the Israel-Palestinian conflict in which their spokespeople take opposing stances. (2023)

4   The Dublin riots of November 2023 revealed a serious strain in the nationalism-multiculturalism tandem. It appears that the Irish population is not as happy about mass immigration and multiculturalism as we all thought and that elements of the urban working class are very angry. (2023)

What's Hecuba to Him?
Brexit and O'Toole

When I read in Fintan O'Toole's overexcited broadside of a book, *Heroic Failure: Brexit and the Politics of Pain* that "the political erotics of imaginary domination and imaginary submission are the deep pulse of the Brexit psychodrama", I was for a moment an envious author resembling the riveted deli customer in *When Harry Met Sally* replying, under fresh circumstances, "I'll have what he's having". And it is but one of many such feverish, inspired and mostly unfalsifiable propositions. Try this: "punk also created the most powerful paradox in the deep neurosis of Brexit: the strange psychic mash-up of revolt and pain, of bondage and freedom, of liberation and self-harm". Or this: "At the heart of the most effective anti-EU stories is oral gratification – and those who would deny it. Brexit's mythologies are all mouth and stomach".

And you naive Leavers out there in UK-land thought you were voting to escape an unelected bureaucracy in Brussels, the 4000 pages (or is it more?) of regulations and (take your pick) the EU common agricultural policy, fisheries laws, freedom of movement policy, ad hoc immigration and refugee rules, or the brewing plans for an armed United States of Europe. How he gets to these lurid conclusions is, of course, Dr O'Toole's entertaining and infuriating book, but just to quote them is to imply the odds against his journey's being convincing. I am a huge admirer of Fintan O'Toole as a literary critic, newspaper columnist, and perceptive cultural historian. But ironically for a book that sees Brexit as malady, there is something disturbingly wayward about *Heroic Failure*.

Like Sally, O'Toole has method in his performance. Brexit for him "is essentially an English phenomenon". "Essentially", not "primarily". (The author is big on getting to the defining nitty-gritty of everything, hence the 1969 comedy *The Italian Job* is "the quintessential English film" – well, certainly for his purposes.) But if the Leave vote in the EU referendum was 52.5% in Wales, 44.2% in Northern Ireland (re-run, that would be much higher, thanks to post-referendum Sinn Féin and their border poll) and 38% in Scotland, surely "essentially" is not the *mot juste*. That's an awful lot of people outside England who voted Leave. One of the two largest vacancies in *Heroic Failure* is the 17 million who voted to get out; their only identity is, by implication, that of useful idiots. It seems mighty insulting to claim that these millions out in the shires and counties had no thoughts of their own but were merely conned by a gang (his word) of Brexiteers into swallowing a "toxic cocktail" (see below).

The other emptiness is the European Union itself (which after all somehow provoked Brexit), the virtues of which are nowhere flaunted in order to prove the madness of Brexit. Instead, the restriction of Brexit to its English essence allows the author to view Brexit as a phenomenon that defines the truest England: "Brexit is at heart an English nationalist project". That can be refined even further: Brexit is a fantasy of the "English reactionary imagination" which he sees as having been at work for centuries (1066 and all that) and – it is his inescapable corollary – is at the very core of Englishness. And that imagination is most active at the idiot apex of society: Brexit is "another upper-class jest" by the poncey English public-school culture. "In keeping with the camp nature of the whole Brexit discourse, [Brexit] is a social class drag act". At the summit we find, unsurprisingly, Boris Johnson and Jacob Rees-Mogg; indeed, as if it were litter on Everest, we find Brexit is somehow emblematized in Boris' empty packet of prawn-flavoured potato crisps. For a man who prides himself on seeing through the conspiracy which he believes Brexit is founded upon (the chief Brexiteers are secretly out to dismantle EU protections of the environment, labour, and social welfare), the author has written us an exposure that looks very like a conspiracy theory itself.

The author tells us that most of the book is new though outgrown from his *Irish Times* articles, but the propulsion of the book stays true to the spirit of the newspaper columns. The writing sparkles (perhaps too dazzlingly) and the general historical knowledge on display is impressively broad-ranging, but O'Toole is in a rush, so much so that the book assumes that Brexit has already happened and has been an unmitigated disaster; this is to take the journalistic scoop to its limits; his *Titanic* has not yet left port. He scorns the English "journalistic hyperventilation" during the "mad cow war" (one of his vivid historical analogies and prologues for Brexit) but like early-stage Sally and the author himself, I too was hyperventilating over many pages of O'Toole's primer of Brexit psychology.

And psychology, not political science, is the "discipline" which drives *Heroic Failure*. England is anthropomorphized as a patient on a couch whom the author diagnoses in order, allegedly, to effect a cure. Any English history adduced in the book is evidence of behaviour betraying a national disorder. The most evident symptom of an inner malaise is self-pity which, we are told in a passage quoted from Herbert Spencer, mixes a sense of self-worth ("implied superiority") and the perception of undeserved treatment from others, which O'Toole melodramatises into a deep sense of grievance and "a high sense of superiority" because he already has the English in his sights. Indeed, within the paragraph the self-pity which somehow drives Brexit has become a fevered *imagining* of "a revolt against intolerable oppression". This characteristic escalation is possible because Brexit is never analysed as the Exit of Great Britain and Northern Ireland from the European Union but instead trips off the keyboard in six letters and is analysed biographically as a man (a white man, a middle-aged or elderly man, an angry man, a racist man, an arrogant man and, I'm afraid, a straw man). We are told that Brexit Man (England, for O'Toole's intents and purposes) wallows in self-pity, suffers the "torment" of being unable to square feelings of inferiority with feelings of superiority, alternates neurotically between sadism and masochism, lives on delusions, courts and celebrates failure, suffers the state of abjection and as 200 pages tell us, engages in all manner of surrogation, transference, displacement and scapegoating. Basket Man, in a word. A somehow living, breathing toxic cocktail.

It is a country-as-patient that once again is exhibiting these sorry and bad-habit conditions, this time through Brexit. Presumably Rees-Mogg and Johnson are not actually candidates for the loony bin, but how can these psychological traits and maladies, which impute a great deal of subjectivity, operate at a national level without the agency of individuals? Surely this was worth clarifying. In the meantime, if Brexit is a person, a villain, indeed, a very Iago (he is also expressly identified as Fortinbras at one point but never as the split-minded Hamlet who is a good guy), then all manner of supporting evidence can be recruited, particularly from novels, several of which are seconded as players in O'Toole's own comic Condition-of-England novel. As though a modest proposal, it's suggested that "It does not seem entirely beside the point that, in the years immediately leading up to Brexit, by far the biggest-selling book by an English author in any genre was E.L. James's *Fifty Shades of Grey*". There follow four pages of analysis of the novel's submission-and-domination dynamic. English author, s & m theme, best-seller: ergo the Zeitgeist, indeed Brexit *n'est ce pas*? But what of the same novel in unmentioned EU-loyal Ireland? Almost half a million books in the *Fifty Shades of Grey* series were sold by 2015, making € 5 million for the author; the first in the series was the 5th ranked Irish best-seller the same year; in one week it sold 24,500 copies. The English (and not just the ones with reactionary imagination) allegedly bought the novel to reinforce their dominance-and-submission habit that would soon be given a real-life work-out in the EU referendum. And the Irish reason for avid purchase?

Cartooning the English when the Irish culturally overlap so amply with them is risky. The author recalls the typical English meal out in the 1980s as starting with prawn cocktail (there follows the vulgarly unappetising recipe): indeed, I remember it well from Dublin dining tables in those years. He is determined to make a meal of prawn cocktail – "the quintessential English idea of fine dining" (as Reagan might have said, "there you go again") – and cites at length Johnson's tongue-in-cheek embattled defence of prawn cocktail flavoured potato crisps against the food Nazis of the EU; he ignores the tongue-in-cheek in favour of emphasising Johnson's opportunism in exploiting a quintessential English piece of naffery, the prawn crisp. But it was Tayto Crisps (Ireland) that invented the first flavoured crisp production process and one of Tayto's best-selling varieties is prawn. (For such a witty man, the author time and again fails to credit with his own quotations the English for their frequent self-mickey-taking, and accepts what is being satirised as solemn evidence of deplorable truth - Johnson's clowning over crisps, Jean Rook's ironic self-portrait of the English in the *Daily Express*, the *Daily Mail*'s reaction to the EU crisps directive: "Der crunch is coming for munchers of the more exotic-favoured crisps". Brexit is said to be, unbeknownst to the English, like *Dad's Army* - but the English *conceived* that self-deprecating comedy!)

It seems that an English cult of heroic failure has been one historical method of marrying masochism with a sense of superiority. In itself, the theme of heroic defeat or failure in English culture through time (borrowed from a book by Stephanie Barczewski), has legs; but it is, of course, merely a part of the structure of feeling not, as O'Toole makes it, intrinsic to English identity and its central load-bearing beam. We get (all of them anticipating Brexit) the evacuation of Corunna, the charge of the Light Brigade, the Franklin expedition, Scott of the Antarctic, Islandlwana, Khartoum, the Somme and the "flight" from Dunkirk – but silence on Wellington and Waterloo, Shackleton, Rorke's Drift (what Brit recalls in preference Islandlwana?), the Battle of Britain, D-Day, Bluebird, the conquest of Everest (an English expedition), Roger Bannister and the 4-minute mile, Wembley 1966. O'Toole complains about a "vertiginous analogy" Daniel Hannan, MEP and Brexiteer, made between the condition of the Irish Free State in 1921 and Brexiting Britain in 2018. But the precedents, prologues and parallels for Brexit in *Heroic Failure* are an unremitting series of vertiginous analogies. One of them is the Hundred Years War (begun in the early 14th century) which is summarised over three pages. What is the connection? Well, England's answer to the problem of military manpower in France: "Its solution was one that would appeal to most of the free-market ultras behind Brexit: the war was privatized and outsourced to gangsters" resulting in "terrorism on a great scale … They stormed towns, raping and killing". With chivalrous bathos we are reassured that "Even the worst Brexit will be nothing like the catastrophe of the Hundred Years War"; for this relief much thanks. But it is still worth recalling, apparently, because the effects of Brexit could last a hundred years, the number of years being the only connection, and a wild surmise at that.

Failure it seems is hardwired into the English psyche and Brexit is more of the same. Worse, it is the spawn of the usual suspect, the Empire. Brexit as nasty imperial nostalgia is a main plank in the author's platform. The decision to withdraw from the EU and seek trading opportunities in the bigger world beyond, with China and India, North America, the south Pacific, to re-orientate the country and in doing so unfetter pent-up energies – these have nothing to do with Brexit: no, Brexit is Little England in the cockpit of Empire, not Big World; the quintessential aim of Brexit is to re-constitute the old white colonies – "putting the old white empire back together again". Perish the thought that apart from vast overseas markets that the UK at present cannot independently exploit there might be practical economic and logistical advantages in trading with partners who share history, a language, and memories of a common culture. Talk about the hermeneutics of suspicion. The author is wildly more conscious of the British Empire than the average Brit Leaver is.

But then retro-imperialism is part and parcel of the problem posed by "The rise of reactionary and xenophobic nationalism in England" to which membership of the EU is the implied solution. Agreed, an English rightward trend is indeed worrying, but does the English right wing begin to compare for extremism and the threat of violence with the right wings in Germany or France, two pillars of the EU? Are there far right-wing parties in the British parliament? (The simultaneous internationalist radical-left turn goes unremarked.) No matter, Brexit is a right-wing movement which is not even centrally about the EU; it is a sublimation of rage, not at EU bureaucracy or increasing loss of national sovereignty, but at black Britons, the sublimation necessitated by the decline of overt racism in England! Heads I win, tails you lose. This free-floating English nastiness simply scoured the land for a new cause to inhabit and happened upon the EU. Would the average Leaver not feel a mite insulted on reading this?

Brexit, then, is a force concealing its aggressive neo-imperialist and ultra right-wing agenda (it wants to exit multiculturalism, feminism, immigration, globalization and Islamism as well as the EU) behind an apparition of its inverse; to succeed, it "needs to imagine that it is a revolt against intolerable oppression". O'Toole sees no oppression at work, just the fantasy of such, nor anything to get worked up about, but at no point does he remind us of the benign workings of the EU that malevolent Brexiteers have distorted for their own deplorable ends. The notorious EU regulations are but "petty annoyances", though in a recent *Irish Times* article by the author (February 12) they are more than outweighed by the bureaucracy from which the EU allegedly *frees* the member nations. (Is this not damning with gossamer faint praise?) In only two pages (pp.130–131) is the EU his real focus and on them he lists only negatives of the EU: its drift from social democracy, its installation of a technocratic elite, the alarming increase in economic inequality, the dastardly treatment of Greece. (The last is page-turningly recounted in Yanis Varoufakis' unmentioned *Adults in the Room*, the most convincing case for Brexit I have read.) Yet for the author, there is no better alternative to the EU. O'Toole says he, like all of us, was warned there is no better alternative *by the EU itself*, which therefore "In the best sense" has been a Project Fear! (More perversely faint praise.) So the UK will get no credit for staring down that fear. He will not champion at any length the virtues of the EU, but merely insist that Brexit is self-harm, in addition to its Trojan horse carrying-capacity for some very bad hombres.

At all costs, the book will not countenance reasonable or mundane explanations for Brexit (whether you then accept them or not), nor the enormous complexity of the ongoing event and of the participants, for and against, who come in all shapes and sizes and from all social classes and backgrounds, with or without other agendas. But O'Toole early on makes a wise observation that ought to have been his starting-point for a patient search for its cause: "As an idea, the EU had a distinctly weak grip on English allegiance" (and, we could add, on a significant portion of Welsh, Northern Irish and Scottish allegiances). Yes, the EU has never been a good fit for the UK. Yet the boredom, indifference or bemusement on the eve of the UK's entry into the Common Market shown by the writers, scholars and commentators whom O'Toole quotes amounted in his opinion to "a treason of the clerks". Perhaps. But what of the virtual unanimity of the current commentariat in Dublin and London, and on all the campuses (now bastions of conformity) in favour of the vast machinery of the EU and its dubious political aspirations? What of their contempt for the people for their "illiberal" views on the EU, multiculturalism, immigration, Islam? Is this blanket orthodoxy, suspect if not smelly, with dissenters despised as reactionary, not also treason of the clerks? (Especially since the clerks often have vested interests, such as tasty EU largesse for scholars.) Orwell is plentifully quoted and it's easy to recruit his musing on the desirability of a democratic socialist united Europe in support of the EU; but something tells me he would have recoiled from a quasi-democratic, Big Brotherish mega-bureaucracy.

Over the decades the allegiance weakened further until a decision was taken to escape from a behemoth-in-progress, a majority decision taken by 17 million citizens, rightly or wrongly, and after a strenuous pre-referendum campaign. It is arguable that we are witnessing with Brexit an astonishing, overheated, even worrisome exercise in democracy – our democracy in full media and social-media cry – but not an undemocratic tussle between a few over-privileged and louche bad guys and the many good guys (though the English anti-Brexit good guys are oddly thin on O'Toole's ground). Those English good guys have, of course, given *Heroic Failure* rave reviews, reflecting the very self-deprecation and tolerance that O'Toole fails to find much evidence of in contemporary England. To complete the irony, it is three impressive commentators of Irish background, living in England, who are strenuously pro-Brexit – Daniel Hannan, Liam Halligan and Brendan O'Neill.

Heroic Failure is by no means O'Toole's last word on Brexit. Between November 2018 and February 2019, I have read and bookmarked at least eleven heated columns by him in the *Irish Times*, some of them I would judge to be sheer Brit-bashing. The preoccupation exceeds the demands of journalistic reportage (these are deeply-engaged and freighted opinion pieces) and hints at a fixation. But since Brexit is a matter for the UK and since - apart from DUP-bashing (plucking low-hanging fruit) - O'Toole shows no more real interest in Northern Ireland than the rest of the Southern Irish intelligentsia, I found myself echoing Hamlet's puzzlement: "What's Hecuba to him, or he to Hecuba?" In his Introduction he says it is amicable concern: "when your neighbour is going mad it is only reasonable to want to understand the source of their distress." But the mocking gibes are too vicious ("The only stiff upper lips on display in England now belong to the victims of botched Botox jobs") and the caricatures too reductive and sometimes cruel, for me to believe that. Something else is going down.

Brexit may have provided a seemingly legitimate opportunity for some venerable reflex anti-Britishness in the South of Ireland. One hopes this is not the explanation for Fintan O'Toole's diatribe, though I fear that this might explain some of the *Schadenfreude*. I am hazarding another explanation, however. I believe the heatedness of *Heroic Failure* and the columns is generated by that of a worried stakeholder's very real investment; Fintan O'Toole, though based in Dublin, is deeply embedded in English culture. His distant models may be Shaw and Wilde who wittily derided the English but who lived among them and were honorary English writers. The tension and contradiction in their identity no longer vexes only those who were called Anglo-Irish. The educated Irish have for decades lived what I call two-passport lives, culturally inhabiting Ireland and England without incongruity - or challenge. Moreover, one thinks of all those Irish entertainers, sportsmen, professors and lecturers, BBC reporters and correspondents who live and work at the heart of British culture, and help that heart pump the blood of the culture, yet oddly have nothing good to say on the intimate Irish-British relationship. O'Toole has rightly given himself permission to explain mockingly the English to themselves because like Wilde and Shaw he not only stands among them but, at the level of educated culture, to flip Byron, is *of* them.

It is Brexit that is laying bare the scope of the investment. Beneath the virtually unanimous revulsion against Brexit in educated Ireland I detect some panic that the two-nation cultural "Schengen" area, the UK and Ireland, is under threat. The panic has provoked the over-reaction. Promoting the EU by lip-service is the current official face of Irishness but it is unconvincing; I have yet to read a heartfelt Irish championing of the EU, and *Heroic Failure* is not it either. The author's personable Introduction recalls his first visit as a boy to an

England that was terrifying and strange despite the fact that he had devoured British comics. The Irish self now looking back sees that the English-Irish relationship was and is extremely complicated and two-way. But the political and social implications of this cultural descant are not here explored, nor are they explored by the educated Irish generally, for whom the cultural *expression* of Irishness must deny the cultural *experience* of being, often seamlessly, of both of these islands. For O'Toole to confine himself to English Brexit instead of exploring UK Brexit was a bright book-making decision but a dimmer cultural decision that passed over a door to a complex inconvenient truth yet to be investigated and explained. The book that he discountenanced would have been the pioneering one. The Irish denial of their deep archipelagic identity was, a century ago or more, perfectly understandable and laudable; the denial had to be made in order to achieve a measure of necessary independence. But over the past half century it has wrought damage on these islands, creating dangerous binary choices, though here is not the place to assess the damage. (I may be more alive to the damage as a Northern Irishman.)

As well as cleverly entertaining and exasperating me, *Heroic Failure* has, I admit, caused me to look twice at Boris Johnson and Jacob Rees-Mogg and some of the more dubious aspects of the Brexit campaign and I thank Fintan O'Toole for that.[1] But because in his peculiar vehemence he has overplayed his hand, what I see as the unacknowledged subtext of his book has convinced me that the longer-term solution to our shared interminable and painful political predicament is a cultural coming-clean, though for the foreseeable future it will be the road not taken in the South of Ireland. (2019)

---

1   As it has happened, Boris Johnson and certain other top Tories deserved O'Toole's cheerful venom more than I judged in 2019, certainly in the matter of Northern Ireland which they have treated with callous abandon. This is the only concession (though not an insignificant one) I can think to make, seven years after the referendum. (2023)

The Story

The silence of the unionists is puzzling and from the academy, deafening. There is a swelling tide of support for a united Ireland with no breakwater in sight. Actually, the breakwater is hiding in plain sight, so huge it has been invisible. It is one that Northern Irish republicans will recognise instantly: The Story.

In *The Cuchullin Saga in Irish Literature* (1898), Eleanor Hull wrote that patriotism "rests upon what we may call the historic imagination. It connects itself with certain events in the past history of our country, or with occurrences ... that have stamped themselves upon the mind of the nation". Hull was confirming the foundation stone for what became the Irish Cultural Revival that in turn nourished the Irish War of Independence.

The historic imagination suffuses everything of public note in the Irish Republic. The 1916 Proclamation, the speeches of the founding martyrs, the flag, the anthem, the 1937 Constitution (despite the 38 amendments until 2019), the anniversaries, the Irish language, Gaelic sports, the pantheon of heroes and the sin-bin of traitors and enemies. Southern Irish education, institutions, government policies, customs, values and worldview – these are all suffused. Ninety-Eight, the Famine, the Diaspora, Easter 1916, the founding of the Free State and Republic – these were the kilns in which Irish nationhood was fired.

The Story in its bare bones is of colonisation and resistance, catastrophes and martyrdom, and the promise of emancipation and unity. Of the feats of martial heroes and the folk wisdom, piety and sufferance of the peasantry. A story of chronic adversity and penultimate triumph pending reunification of the homeland in an all-island republic. A story written from the moral high-ground from a marginalised perspective and engendering a free-floating and, because it is a narrative of incompleteness, an understandable sense of entitlement. The Story has underwritten the extraordinary sympathy extended wholesale to Catholic or native Ireland by much of the world, a sympathy that in the cases of specific historical events has sometimes been misdirected, to the detriment of those who have been on the business end of the Story. It has ensured a steady flow of chits from matron, to turn an English public school phenomenon into a metaphor for allowances and exemptions. It was O'Grady who established as a theme in the Story Irish exceptionalism, the uniqueness of Ireland. This is in no way to underestimate the real historical suffering of poverty and suppression endured by the Catholic Irish over centuries.

Nevertheless, *in the light of the present and recent past and the repeated desire for unification*, the Story is well past its tell-by date.

The Story was briefly interrupted in the 1980s by "revisionist" Southern historians, but soon righted itself by what folklorists call Anderson's Law of Self-Correction. For the Story is a law unto itself, very nearly an autonomous entity. It dictates the reality its tellers are to see, instead of reality revising the story. It can conduct not just sentiments but also policies and political interpretations. The Story, for example, wrote Fintan O'Toole's recent anti-Brexit book, *Heroic Failure*, which is why it is an anti-English outburst, a work of bizarre ventriloquism. Brexit has been a convenient pretext for a re-telling of the Story by the Dublin commentariat, inserting economics and current politics into it where called on.

That recent radical changes in Irish society involving divorce, gay marriage, abortion, EU membership, immigration and the emptying pews of the Catholic Church have not seriously altered or enlarged the Story is testament to its resilience. It still reiterates, and not quite *sotto voce*, that England is the enemy and northern unionists are strangers in their midst (Yeats set the tone there), who must be made to see sense, leave their nation and dwell in an entirely different one (by a kind of forced marriage if necessary).

The Story is a stirring and addictive narrative. But it is not my story, though I know it well and as a youth was enamoured of it. After those youthful days of an extracurricular romance with Irishness, I realised that mine is the British story, and the Irish Story, as it is written (and sung), cannot accommodate it. And mine is not just the Ulster Scots (Scotch-Irish) story, though that, too, is stirring if not addictive, but the entire British chronicle. Fifty years of studying Irish culture, and latterly my "lived experience", have confirmed for me that as well as being Irish I am British, bit and bundle, thumb and thimble. Should the UK break asunder and the skies fall, my primary kinship would still be across the narrow water. For geography is irrelevant: try telling Alaskans, separated from their country-folk in the lower 48 by 800 kilometres through the Yukon and British Columbia, that they should logically be Canadians - then duck.

These Stories generate a deep ecology: they enter not just the hearts and minds, but the viscera. Most Irish have internalised their Story (as I have mine) and believe it to be indubitable.

So what is the solution to the narrative deadlock on this island? I'm now convinced that only the Southern Irish can provide it.

Fianna Fáil Senator Mark Daly wants to convene New Ireland Forum 2 in order to dispel unionist fears of what he considers the inevitable united Ireland. But the fact that Senator Daly's office "is awash with nationalist emblems", as a recent profile tells us, shows that the Story is convening his Forum. I suggest he convene instead a New Ireland Forum in nationalist privacy that explores the intimate mutual relations between the Republic and the UK and thinks of unionists as fellow dwellers on the island and in the archipelago with a quite different Story. And subject his Story to an assessment as to its authority and writ and to its relevance to present reality. Let brains be cudgelled to write a new and inclusive Story that doesn't simply narrate Ulster-British culture or the Irish in Britain as addenda but instead rewrites the whole, if only (for the task to be feasible) since the years of massive, voluntary migration from the twenty-six counties to Britain in the 1950s and 1960s. This would at long last shift the burden of self-examination from harassed unionists to nationalists. Southern nationalists, at no cost, have assumed that the tide of history flows from north to south on the island, instead of admitting that it flows between the two islands. And that the interdependency of the UK and Ireland is asymmetrical and greatly in favour of the latter.

I can even suggest some panellists from England to help with the rewrite: Eamon Duffy, Roy Foster and Bernard O'Donoghue of Oxbridge; the journalists Mary Kenny, Brendan O'Neill and Liam Halligan; the writer Edna O'Brien; Daniel Hannan MEP and Conor McGinn MP; TV entertainers Graham Norton and Dara Ó Briain; Orla Guerin, Joe Lynam and Fergal Keane of the BBC. These sample figures work at the heart of British culture and help keep the blood of that heart pumping. How, they could be asked, is the Irish Story to be read in the light of their own long and distinguished lives in Great Britain? This Forum would reassure unionists that any discussion of a united Ireland is not simply a vehicle for predestined Irish separatism. And it would liberate Southerners from a Story so captivating it even dictates the country's foreign policy.

It might also reassure unhappy Northern nationalists that they are not marooned in the UK, that Southerners, too, are inextricably entangled in the culture of the archipelago and that we all belong to these two magnificent islands.

But, meanwhile, it is "Now read on" with the Story. Leo Varadkar has suggested that April 18, 1949 – the day the Free State became the Republic – be annually commemorated each Easter Monday, when the Easter rebellion is already commemorated. Bad linkage if you dream of unification.

Entitled the Irish are to tell their Story, and they tell and sing it well and with gusto. But when the Taoiseach says that "Our history shows that symbols matter, dreams matter", he needs to remember that unionists have their symbols and dreams, too, just as potent and no less legitimate. In a New Ireland Forum 2, we could finally show the huge positive overlap in the Stories of these two islands. (2019/2023)

Solace from Aughnacloy

Under pandemic lockdown I have derived a great deal of comfort and optimism from my re-acquaintance with a now forgotten author, James Harpole. I recently bought the 1947 thirtieth edition of *The Surgeon's Log: Impressions of the Far East* (1911), a hot seller for decades. It is a marvellous account of his short time as a young ship's doctor on a cargo vessel bound for Egypt, Malaya and Japan.

Harpole in the course of his life was a civilian and army surgeon, novelist, broadcaster and essayist who gathered along the way a DSO, CBE and Serbian knighthood. Harpole was the most celebrated medical populariser of his day.

"Harpole", he explained in his engrossing autobiography, *Surgeon's Journey* (1957), was a pen-name, made necessary because medical etiquette back then forbade doctors engaging under their own names in anything that could be regarded as self-advertising. His practice was between Harley and Wimpole streets, hence Harpole.

Harpole was in fact J. Johnston Abraham (1876–1963) over whose name *Surgeon's Journey* was published. His family came from Aughnacloy in County Antrim and his earliest memory was of watching (before approval or disapproval were relevant) the ritual burning of Robert Lundy's effigy from the window of his Coleraine home. (Lundy was the Governor of Londonderry who, in sympathy with the enemy, failed to defend the city against the Catholic troops of James II during the Siege of Derry, 1688–89.)

Abraham's father was a tea-merchant, his grandfather a linen merchant. His people were Primitive Methodists despite the Jewish-sounding name and he grew up fluent in braid Scots. But Abraham's pride of ancestry was without rancour, as such pride usually is in those who travel the world. Besides, his medical reading of history lent him an even-handed humanity we in Ireland still need to learn. He knows the besieged in Derry died in their thousands of typhus fever, diphtheria and dysentery, but knows too that King James's army was likewise decimated by disease and melted away.

At Trinity College Dublin he studied both literature and science, as one could once do, but on the advice of the celebrated Shakespearian scholar Edward Dowden, opted for the security of a profession. That choice did not prevent him from soon writing a novel that became a *succès de scandale*. *The Night Nurse* (1913), recreating the avid private desires and ambitions of nurses and young doctors, was banned by hospital matrons in every English hospital save Guy's in London and sold promiscuously. Abraham may have been the best-selling Northern Irish author of the twentieth century. He was elected member of the Athenaeum, became a friend of Rudyard Kipling and met D.H. Lawrence.

Abraham chose to be a surgeon over a physician, and he proved to be a skilled and venturesome one. He recalls for us some hairy moments, such as retrieving a service knife out of sight in the pericardium, the bag-like membrane that encloses the heart, plunged there by a suicidal Great War soldier in Egypt who had convicted himself of cowardice. The soldier survived the operation but died days later (of typhus), not an unfamiliar story in medical annals, it seems.

Though a surgeon, Abraham's posts in hospitals in Dublin, London and overseas involved him in epidemics of bacterial and viral diseases of the kind we all now face. He admitted his fear of tetanus, and when he served with the British Red Cross Serbian Mission in the Great War he saw it kill soldier after soldier horribly. He was equally afraid of typhoid fever which he watched ravage the Royal

Irish Constabulary when he was with Dr Steeven's Hospital in Dublin. In Serbia during the Great War Austrian prisoners died in thousands before the epidemic spread to the civilian population. He was in the midst of the London smallpox epidemic of 1902, having been familiar with the disease in Dublin where it was not uncommon.

Engaged with the Royal Army Medical Corps in Egypt towards the end of the Great War, Abraham fought malaria as well as diphtheria and typhus. But even those menaces paled beside the great influenza pandemic of 1918–19 when the base hospitals in Palestine were overwhelmed and casualty clearing stations had to hoard their patients.

Surgeon's Journey reminds us of our human vulnerability to the ills that flesh is heir to. All adults are presently being taught this fearsome lesson. Yet it is a story too of inspiring drama that we too are now being witness to: the drama of testing, diagnosis, containment, treatment and intervention, and, fingers crossed, cure.

But as time goes on, fingers need to be crossed less frequently. We are now aware of who the utterly necessary professionals are in our midst. We should become aware of how this expertise - the diagnostic and healing powers – came into being. Abraham in the course of his autobiography tells us what extraordinary medical introductions, procedures and breakthroughs he witnessed during his career. Appendectomies; X-rays; surgical masks; dedicated operating tables; inoculation for diphtheria; serum for tetanus; penicillin; vaccination for typhoid; the discovery of hormones; the cure for rickets, and so on.

Above all, or so it seems to us, though less obviously to Mr Abraham, was the creation of the UK National Health Service in 1948. He writes of doctors being in "the throes of negotiating" with a socialist government over the terms of the National Health Act of 1947 and of "the shadow" of the coming NHS falling over the hospitals. (This disagreement and ambivalence about the NHS has been revived during our Covid ordeal.)

But the private system that had lasted for centuries was coming to an end. We in the United Kingdom know what a triumph the creation of the NHS was, at least for decades, and how in our own throes of the Coronavirus it must be repaired and cherished. It was the nationalisation that was in the air after the war that made temperamentally conservative doctors in private practices apprehensive, but Abraham admits that his own fears proved to be greatly exaggerated.

Surgeon's Journey, like Abraham's other fascinating books drawn from his extensive medical casebook, is a story of painstaking detective work, but also of resolve, action and energy. How timely it is to read of the scarcity of hospital beds under canvas on the eve of the third Battle of Gaza in the Great War in 1917. Between sunset and dawn, within earshot of the opening salvoes, the RAMC readied 3000 beds up and under cover for the expected casualties.

No wonder Harpole-Abraham called one of his volumes of memoirs *The White-Coated Army* (1938). He saw doctors (and we can now add nurses) as "officers in a health army fighting the long fight against disease". Under lockdown, I appreciate that thought infinitely more than when I first read it.[1] (2020)

---

1   I discuss Abraham's books in my study, *Irish Novels 1890–1940: New Bearings in Culture and Fiction* (Oxford, 2008).

Ireland out of England?

One
Sharon Horgan, 49, grew up on a turkey farm in Meath and moved to London in her early twenties in pursuit of an acting career. She worked in a job centre in Kilburn before recording sketches for a BBC radio pilot. Breakthrough success came when she wrote and starred in the BBC sitcom *Pulling*, after which she wrote *Divorce* for Sarah Jessica Parker. She married an English property developer and lives with her daughters Sadhbh and Amer in a designer house in Hackney, where in fact she was born to a Kildare mother and Irish-New Zealand father. The actress and ITV presenter Laura Whitmore was born in Dublin and educated by the nuns at Loreto Bray and now lives in Camden, wife of a Scottish comedian. Genevieve O'Reilly's family left Dublin for Australia when she was ten but since 2005 the 43 year-old actress of *Star Wars* and *Tin Star* fame has made her home in east London with her chiropractor husband. Niamh Algar, 27, left her Mullingar home in 2017, headed to London, and landed a starring role in the Channel 4 miniseries, *The Virtues*. She will better that with the English director Ridley Scott's big-budget series, *Raised by Wolves*. Algar is now house-hunting in London.

Paul Mescal from Maynooth is not at the house-hunting stage quite yet, having moved to London just before the Coronavirus lockdown to star in BBC's *Normal People*. Alex Murphy and Chris Walley, both from Cork, star in the BBC comedy series *The Young*

Offenders, and its British audience proves, as it does with Channel 4's *Father Ted* and BBC Scotland's *Mrs Brown's Boys,* that it regards the Irish as culturally outlier versions of themselves. Keith Duffy from Dublin has copper-fastened that perception by playing an outlier character in that most British of television programmes, *Coronation Street.* Duffy's initial success came as a singer in Boyzone alongside Ronan Keating from Dublin who now hosts a show on London's Magic Radio. Keating was managed for some years by Louis Walsh from Co. Mayo who achieved his highest profile with ITV's *X-Factor.*

Horgan, Algar, Whitmore and Mescal are only the most recent aspiring southern Irish movie, stage and television performers trooping to London. The Wexford actress Charlie Murphy left for London in 2013 after success in a BBC drama; she was reported to be in a long-term relationship with Ciaran O'Brien, the Irish stage actor also living in London. They followed in the footsteps of Kate Binchy, Donal Donnelly, Richard Harris, Peter O'Toole (born either in Connemara or Leeds), Eddie Byrne, John Welsh, Peter Caffrey, Bernadette O'Farrell from Birr (ITV's Maid Marian to Richard Greene's Robin Hood), Cyril Cusack, Pierce Brosnan (born in Drogheda, taken to Britain aged eleven and later enrolled the Drama Centre in London), Fiona Shaw CBE, Sinéad Cusack, Cillian Murphy, Andrew Scott, Killian Donnelly, and Daragh O'Malley who grew up in Limerick and became friends with Harris, a fellow Limerick-man; O'Malley found his place in the thespian sun by starring in *Sharpe,* the ITV series, after learning the ropes at the London Academy of Music and Dramatic Art; he married in London. Byrne was a congenial presence in British movies in my youth and whereas the usual sites have him born in Dublin in 1911, his birthplace on PeoplePill.com is given as Birmingham, with his upbringing in the Irish capital. The doubling of Byrne's native countries, as in the cases of O'Toole, Brosnan and Horgan, is telling. And John Welsh played English characters so impeccably in *The Forsyte Saga, Vanity Fair* and *The Moonstone,* among numerous other dramas, that I was surprised to discover that he was born John James Walsh in Wexford in 1914.

The curve of actors' visibility goes north or south, but a select few entertainers become celebrities which means they settle in with the showbusiness equivalent of a professorial chair, and become national identities, in the Australian sense of the word. I grew up in the ubiquitous sunny presence of Eamonn Andrews CBE because my father won a TV in a works prize draw as early as 1954. He was born in Synge Street Dublin, educated by the Christian Brothers at Synge Street School, and was a sports commentator for Radio Éireann before graduating to the BBC in London. His most famous role was compère of the evergreen *This is Your Life*. Andrews was succeeded as a cheerful fixture in the British consciousness by Terry Wogan - (Sir) Terence Wogan KBE, DL (Deputy Lieutenant, a Crown appointment), son of a Limerick store manager. Now it is Graham Norton from Bandon, the third Irish star in the BBC firmament over the past continuous sixty years, subject of a 2013 *Daily Telegraph* profile, "The making of a national treasure", the nation in question being the UK. Meanwhile, Robert "Sir Bob" Geldof KBE and Freeman of the City of London, born and raised in Dun Laoghaire, is a kind of roving celebrity-campaigner who lives in Battersea but is too divisive to be a national treasure. He can affix KBE to his name but cannot call himself Sir Robert because the Republic of Ireland is not in the Commonwealth; but others call him Sir Bob anyway, no doubt because they know that Ireland does not need to be in the Commonwealth in order to be in the British Isles; Sir Bob is one of them, even when ornery.

What does Irish talent's homing instinct that locks on to London like a heat-seeking missile tell us? Well, at least this: the performative genius of the Irish, if it is also ambitious, needs a metropolis in which to take wing. London (not Dublin, Paris or Berlin) is the metropolis of Ireland. And London, metropolis or not, is in England. The stand-up comedian, Ed Byrne, from Swords, Co. Dublin, graduated from the University of Strathclyde, and then began his career in Glasgow.

He appears often on ITV and the BBC and lives in Essex, a stone's throw from the metropolis. He is quoted in the *Irish Independent* of July 19, 2023 as saying "I don't think if I'd stayed in Ireland I'd be a comedian". Whether that would have been the case for his legendary predecessor Dave Allen (née David Tynan O'Mahony) from Dublin we shall never know as after his father died when he was twelve, his English mother took her sons to England where from the mid-1960s Allen forged a brilliant career, chiefly courtesy of the BBC and his own laid-back, bar-room style, cigarette and whiskey glass in hand. In his comic monologues, he moved easily between subversive observations of English and Irish life. As Mary Kenny the Irish journalist has been in the past few years, Allen was a supple bridge across the troubled waters between the two islands.

Dave Allen was given early exposure on the BBC TV show, *Date with Doonican*. Val Doonican, born in Waterford in 1927, moved to England when he was 24 and joined a musical group that became backing singers in the BBC radio serial *Riders of the Range* that my brothers and I, suckers for all things western, listened raptly to in the early 1950s in Belfast. He broke away as a solo performer with his own laid-back style (wearing a cardigan like an afterthought and crooning from a rocking chair), like Allen becoming a perennial much loved by the British audiences. He spent his last years in Knotty Green, Buckinghamshire. Allen and Doonican were contemporaries of the Dubliners who formed the singing trio, the Bachelors, who were often tiny pleasant-sounding marionettes on the black and white screen of our 12" Bush set after they moved to London from Dublin and never returned.

The singer Róisín Murphy, born and raised in Arklow, moved with her parents to Manchester, stayed when her parents returned to Ireland, and has made a glittering career and life there, with a daughter by the English artist Simon Henwood. We are told that, like many thousands, and quite naturally, "Murphy shares her time between London and Ireland". Why didn't this give the Irish at home pause during their vocal anti-British sentiment during Brexit? Have

Murphy and others felt reciprocal anti-Irish feeling in England? *Au contraire*: warm British-Irish relations in entertainment and the professions have for a century been deliberately bracketed off by Irish politicians and commentators so that the rest of the countless British-Irish relations can be portrayed as inherently and exclusively hostile. We in these islands are in dire need of a candid exposure of those warm relations so that we can then consider how we might import empirical reality into Irish official and unofficial attitudes to the UK and the Union, and encourage a sea-change in Irish popular and political mindset. I believe that the peace of Ireland, the capacity to reconcile the peoples of the archipelago (and then, *and only then*, the people of Ireland itself), depends upon it.

And this is the case because, contrary to what is assumed, neither "the North" nor partition is the chief source of contention between Britain and Ireland. Northern Ireland, in reality, is the veronica that distracts the Irish bull from his real problem which is the British-Irish relationship itself. This schizophrenic relationship would rankle even if the Northern Irish disappeared. Edna Longley's eloquent notion of Northern Ireland as a corridor between Ireland and Britain once seemed hopeful[1], but ambitious Southerners prefer direct traffic with the British mainland and have no interest in the North as a detour, bridge or go-between.

Two

To kick-start this candid exposure, we might read the Irish historian Diarmaid Ferriter's contribution to a recent book, *Britain and Ireland: Lives Entwined. Shifting Borders, Shifting Identity* (2019), which despite its title does not even begin to build on Ferriter's revelations. "Over the last 30 years I have spent more time in London than Belfast and that is not unusual for my peers," writes Ferriter. Indeed; his peers' eyes are fixed firmly on England. Ferriter introduced me to an acronym for the Irish of his generation who live across the water: NIPPLE (new Irish professional people living in England). They are the latest instalment of a very old sequence but more likely than their immediate predecessors to share the culture of their host society. Some of Ferriter's historical statistics are startling. By 1830, Irish soldiers "were estimated to represent 42.2 per cent of the regular British Army ... By 1878 a fifth of all British Army officers were Irish. More than 200,000 Irishmen fought in the First World War and were volunteers rather than conscripts ... at least 60,000 Southern Irish citizens served [in the Second World War] ... Joining the British Army was a family tradition for many, and was not seen by them as either pro-British or anti-Irish". That became "an inconvenient truth", says Ferriter with some understatement.

So inconvenient that President Higgins omitted to mention it in his recent diatribe against the British Empire in which by his account the Irish were exclusively victims of imperial oppression. He also forgot to mention that, as Mary Kenny reminded readers of *The Oldie* recently, the British Empire was very good for the Irish Catholic church; "the Irish missions often tended to follow where the British flag had led," she writes in *Goodbye to Catholic Ireland* (1997). In the 20th century, Ferriter tells us, "1.6 million Irish left for Britain, more than twice as many as went to North America". Roy Foster reminds us in *Paddy and Mr Punch* (1993) that the Irish-born population in Britain in 1861 was 805,000; the combined first-generation and their immigrant parents would have boosted the figure to several million. By 2001, the Irish-born population was 850,000; after all, by the late 1950s, nearly 60,000 Irish were arriving in Great Britain annually. (These last figures courtesy of Maurice Sweeney's moving 2009 documentary set in Birmingham, *The Forgotten Irish*.)

Obviously many of the descendants of the three million Irish who have emigrated to Britain since 1600 (Ferriter's figure), have simply dissolved into the mainstream of British society, helping to feed and propel that stream while, in many cases, keeping proudly alive at some level of acknowledgement their Irish ancestry. As we know from David Fitzpatrick's essential study, "A Curious Middle Place:

the Irish in Britain, 1871–1921" (in *The Irish in Britain, 1815–1939*, eds. Swift and Sheridan), by the turn of the twentieth century many Irish had escaped the Irishtowns of Liverpool, Manchester and other British cities and were moving to the suburbs; they also lived in Stafford, Stockport, Winchester, York, Dundee, Newcastle, Hull, Bristol and other smaller British towns and cities.

The alienation from British culture that first characterised Irish life in Britain accordingly diminished. Foster reminds us of the nineteenth-century Irish "who saw much of their focus and most of their career opportunity as lying across St George's Channel. But for many of the Victorian Irish middle class, life was spent travelling back and forth across the Irish Sea, observing and participating in British forms of Government, reading English books, attending British educational institutions, looking for employment within the structures of the British Empire and speaking English". He refers to those Irish "who went to England and made a good thing out of it"; but we don't need to trumpet the success stories that he tells: a mere reminder of the Irish educated middle-class presence in England is sufficiently novel, and the fact sufficiently unappetising ideologically to many Irish historians, politicians and journalists. But of course, high-profile success stories pack a greater punch than common or garden success stories, and both kinds can help to counterbalance the prevailing lazy image to this day of the Irish in England - exiled, unhappy, discriminated against, nostalgic for the old sod.

During the research for my study, *Irish Novels, 1890–1940: New Bearings in Culture and Fiction* (Oxford University Press, 2008), I was astonished to recover from obscurity so many popular Irish novelists, mostly women and middle class, Catholic and Protestant, who lived in England and set their fiction in either of the two islands, who frequented the Irish mail train and Holyhead ferry between Euston and Dun Laoghaire (or who travelled the Empire) and who wrote in blithe disregard for the nationalist stipulations of the Irish Revival culture-givers. They could be disapproved of ideologically (and have been by Irish critics for a century) *but there they were,* unembittered and more Irish than Patrick Pearse, Erskine Childers, Maud Gonne or Éamon de Valera. Even so, Irish scholars have no intention of dislodging the Irish Revival as the literary counterpart of Irish political nationalism.

Fitzpatrick reminds us that Irishmen were indeed over-represented among casual and seasonal workers, dock labourers and coal heavers, and Irishwomen in domestic service: "In England, Paddy (and doubtless Biddy) remained proletarian". And they remained so into the 1950s. To balance the longstanding discrimination that these particular Irish suffered, Ferriter reminds us of the inimitable opportunities England offered to those who could find no work in Ireland. England was Ireland's missing construction site. Which reminds me. "Oh mother dear, I'm over here," sings the narrator of "McAlpine's Fusiliers", "I never will come back". The song lists what lightens the navvies' nights and induces them to throw their suitcases away: "What keeps me here?/The rake of beer,/The ladies and the crack". Pleasure and freedom, in short. But the image persisted of an oppressed workforce amidst an alien host population. Sweeney's *The Forgotten Irish* reveals how immigrant Irish workers were in fact often exploited by their compatriots who had become contractors in England. And in the song it is the Irish gaffer, The Horseface Toole, who when The Bear O'Shea is killed on site callously retorts "I'm a navvy short". Besides, the navvies weren't press-ganged and trafficked to England. If they were forced to emigrate to Great Britain from Ireland, by whom were they forced? In the cases of the Birmingham Irish that Sweeney profiles in *The Forgotten Irish*, it was to escape hardship, cruelty and sexual abuse in the industrial schools that they absconded to Britain. This was a traumatising experience for some and some suffered homesickness and, in their inner-city loneliness, alcoholism; theirs can be heartbreaking stories. Thirty-five to 40% of the boys who survived institutions in Ireland decamped to Britain, Sweeney tells us. Many rooted themselves in England. We accompany one of his survivors on his return to Baltimore, Cork after decades away. "I'm patriotic," he says, "I love Ireland. But I'm going back to Birmingham. I'm going home".

Subtending this false notion of chronic exploitation of all the Irish in Britain was the claim of the essential *difference* between the British and the Irish as well as an unjust imbalance between oppressor and oppressed. The cultural difference had to be true and deep if it were to justify the separatist agenda of the early 20th century. That agenda, Foster claims, was subscribed to less by Irish living in England than by those radicals who were actually English such as Gonne, Childers, Aodh de Blácam (Hugh Blackham), Charlotte Despard. We learn from Fitzpatrick that in the later 19th century, "Nationalist organizers struggled hard to involve immigrants in the concerns of Ireland and her politics ... Most immigrants avoided all Irish organizations". They were clearly too busy getting on with their lives, though there was later involvement in the Home Rule movement and, as we know from Yeats, an expatriate enthusiasm for Irish drama and literature in Southwark and elsewhere that fed into the incipient cultural revival. But the image that came to prominence was of an Irish population in England in half-voluntary bondage, whose tribulations ("No blacks, no Irish") helped to justify the cause of complete separation of the two countries, culturally as well as politically.

Two sides to the story of the Irish in Britain were indirectly revealed in the Forgotten Irish Campaign that was launched in London in 2007 by President Mary McAleese. It was spearheaded by Peter Sutherland, a businessman and lawyer of Scots ancestry born in Foxrock and who rose to be Attorney General of Ireland, Chairman of Allied Irish Banks and Special UN Representative for International Migration. Queen Elizabeth made him an honorary Knight Commander. He lived in London but at the end returned to Dublin where he died. The campaign was to raise funds and awareness of the elderly Irish in Great Britain who had left Ireland from the 1950s. The campaign manifesto (available online) said they "paved the way for more recent generations of Irish immigrants to

Britain – for people like us". So the thousands of successful Irish professionals in Britain were asked to help those working-class predecessors who had not fared so well. Ironically, the Irish in Britain, especially if successful, have been less understandably, sometimes wilfully, forgotten by those Irish still at home, and where a political party that nourishes itself, and starves others, on its anti-Britishness, is sadly popular.

How well the Irish are doing in Great Britain was revealed by the recent Sewell Commission on Race and Ethnic Disparities which found that the average earnings of the "white Irish" exceeded those of "white British" and that "white Irish unemployment was relatively low". This good news is hardly likely to be trumpeted in the republican mouthpiece, *An Phoblacht*. My only reservation about the happy news is in the concept of "white Irish" as an ethnic group. In "Let's Celebrate Irish Success in Britain," a St Patrick's Day 2021 article in *Spiked*, Rakib Ehsan claims that the success of one ethnic group in Britain, the Catholic Irish, is "oft-overlooked" in debates over race and culture. In order laudably to disprove white homogeneity, he suggests ways in which the Irish are culturally different from white British, which differences explain their success. (But that must have sounded too odd to him, so Ehsan tags on the oppression of the Irish Travellers.) In fact, success at the levels I have been referencing (the professions, the arts, the services, the media) is culturally homogeneous; that is why Irish success in Britain is "oft-overlooked" by the British (as well as by Irish nationalists) – the Irish on those levels are invisibly at home in Britain.

The career of Vincent Keaveny CBE, KStJ is a case in point. After graduating as a bachelor of civil law from University College Dublin, he left for London in 1889 at the age of twenty-four and re-qualified as a financial lawyer in the 1990s. He was elected as a London alderman in 2013, became a City of London sheriff and then, after taking the oath of loyalty to the Crown, took office as London's 693rd Lord Mayor in 2021. He describes himself as "an Irishman, holding an ancient office at the heart of these extraordinary events

– the death of Queen Elizabeth II and coronation of King Charles III". He recalls it as "striking that my nationality was so little remarked upon in the City".[2] That he is "white Irish", a somehow visible and audible minority member in their midst, is something that couldn't, and therefore wouldn't, have occurred to the distinguished British around him.

In order to achieve even Home Rule, it was, of course, necessary to promote difference between Ireland and Britain, not similarity or shared experience, and this is understandable. After all, one inescapable difference was in the fact that the citizens of one country did not unanimously accept rule by the other country, to put it mildly. But whereas Home Rule would have allowed the Irish in Britain to maintain without reproof their British Isles existence, the republican campaign that climaxed in the Easter rebellion necessarily called that existence into question. After 1922, many Irish in Britain must have felt cut adrift. Those in Ireland who wished to join their compatriots across the water, or were judged to be too British in behaviour or belief, were now "West Britons" or "shoneens" and the insult was extended to those Irish in Britain who drew attention to themselves. Were Shaw and Wilde even Irish writers, really? When I was an undergraduate in the 1960s in Belfast, the answer was still No. The Irish in Britain became an unspoken-of population, unless they were McAlpine's fusiliers or equivalent "victims". Unspoken of, and unspeaking, by and large. The Provisional IRA war of the 1970s and 1980s was conducted in England not on behalf of, but despite, the majority of the Irish who lived there.

Yet if we recruit Ferriter's experience, along with the facts of present-day Irish in Britain, the idea of deep separation is patently absurd. But what is the best cultural and policy-form by which the reality of the British-Irish connection can be expressed? No extant policy, political initiative, or major cultural organisation supplies the need. It is a hard question because we are dealing with a network, a web, not alas (or yet), a potential coherent lobby in Britain either of the Irish-born or the British-born Irish; nor is there advocacy back in Ireland. But answers are necessary if we are finally to lay the by-now sorry and reiterative quarrel to rest.

Three

A recurring figure in Ferriter's essay is Kevin Maher whom the scholar would visit in London where Maher lived, and for a time in Camden like many Irish. They shared "a deep-rooted republicanism with a fascination with the activities of the House of Windsor". Ferriter was best man when Maher married a Kensington woman from a Tory family. As it happens, I got my information about the actress Niamh Algar chiefly from an interview with her in the London *Times* of February 29, 2020 by Kevin Maher. Maher is from Dublin but left for London in 1994 when he was 22 to find success as a journalist. He did so, for he is now film critic of the *Times* and has worked as a researcher for Channel 4's *Film Night*. Two novels of his have been published by a London house. He lives in Hertfordshire. His kids, he says, are half Irish/half English "so I'm really suspicious of nationalism" – in other words, of any attempt to impose an Ireland-Britain binary; he is one of the few Irish in England apparently willing to question on the record, even indirectly, the *raison d'être* of Irish republicanism.

In turn, I got my information about Maher chiefly from an April 2013 interview with him in the *Spectator* (a mouthpiece for England *par excellence*, one might think) by J.P. O'Malley, a resourceful freelance journalist from Dublin who left for London in 2009 and has also written for *The Economist* and *The Daily Beast*. Despite the English outlets for his journalism, O'Malley does not appear to share Maher's suspicion of nationalism and regards life in London as responsible for silencing the Irish national narrative; writing about the Irish in London has given him a greater sense of himself as Irish, he says. ("Culture can provide home away from home for Irish in London", *Irish Times*, 14 November, 2014.) But none of this negates the fact of O'Malley's living in the capital of England which in the arts and publishing (and other fields) is also the capital of Ireland.

One can feel, or adopt, the identity of an expatriate in England while daily living the life of a resident, inside or outside the loose company of tens of thousands of one's compatriots. It's a different way of being Irish in Britain. Yet another way, made possible by shuttle flights and encouraged in the beginning, no doubt, by the UK's EU membership, is to be part of what airport staff call "the Monday-morning mob" of Irish commuter-migrant professionals whose work week is spent in a British city and whose weekends are back in Ireland (www.irishpost.com, March 7, 2014).

And how you live as Irish in Britain is now up to you, as the experience of the actress Siobhán McSweeney of *Derry Girls* suggests. After she graduated from University College Cork, she told the *Sunday Times* (Dublin) of May 3, 2020, she enrolled in the Central School of Speech and Drama in London in 2001. What is crucial to remember is how natural those footsteps are that lead from Ireland to Britain. When she moved from Brockley to Kilburn ("County Kilburn, they call it, because there are so many Irish there"), having come from Celtic Tiger Ireland, "I wasn't that keen on bacon and cabbage; and I didn't have the immigrant mindset, because, in my head, I wasn't one: I was just over in London. The idea I had moved from home hadn't occurred to me". She did not regard herself, obviously, as "white Irish". She was just a migrant, not an immigrant from another land. The accidental geography once she was in a certain London neighbourhood meant she *chose* to embrace the ideas of diaspora, enclave and home away from home, where if you are a professional you describe yourself as "based in London" or "currently living in London" (a formula to disguise a commitment to life in England) rather than "living and making my livelihood and career in London", which you are. Now, she says, "I'm a fully paid-up member of the immigrant community: I break down and weep in the supermarket at the sight of Tayto crisps and Kimberley and Mikado biscuits." But with her wit, self-awareness, talent and success, McSweeney is unlikely to join the old forgotten Irish. There is role-playing here, surely, for she is clearly a NIPPLE, a new Irish professional person living in England.

There are of course other high-profile Irish journalists and commentators living and working in England besides Maher and O'Malley, including Mary Kenny from Dublin; John Naughton from Mayo (also a research fellow at the University of Cambridge); Melanie McDonagh from Wicklow (happily writing for both the *Spectator* and the *Catholic Herald*); Gerard O'Donovan from Cork (*Daily Telegraph*); Laura Perrins, a law graduate from UCD and co-editor of *Conservative Woman*; Helen Joyce from Dublin (PhD from Cambridge, writing for the *Economist*) and John O'Ceallaigh ("luxury travel journalist" who is "based in London", according to his website). Besides being a journalist, Kevin Maher is a novelist, only one of the many Irish writers living in England, including Ruth Dudley Edwards, Jean Casey, Edna O'Brien, Gerard O'Donovan (the same), Caroline O'Donoghue, Declan Ryan, Martina Evans, Olivia Kiernan, Megan Nolan, the late Josephine Hart from Mullingar, who died in 2011 as Lady Saatchi, and their myriad illustrious predecessors since the Revival, including George Moore, Sean O'Casey, AE and W.B. Yeats. Other Irish writers, such as Marian Keyes from Limerick, spent their creatively formative years in London, where Keyes married an Englishman. Niamh Mulvey from Kilkenny spent formative years in London where she worked with distinction in publishing for ten years and will join the ranks of Irish writers in 2022 with a short story collection from Picador; her London agent is Sallyanne Sweeney from Dublin.

Indeed, so many Irish writers are in the Big Smoke that Tony Murray, a first-generation London-Irishman who teaches at the London Metropolitan University, started the Irish Writers in London Summer School in 1996. Murray catches first- and second-generation London-Irish writers in his net, and they could include, of course, John Walsh, Martin McDonagh and Brendan O'Neill (and before them, J.G. Farrell). The multi-talented Helen Mullane lives in Sweden but is from north London and flies the Irish flag when she races dog-sleds, as RTE is delighted to remind us. In an

Oldie column, Mary Kenny defended Edna O'Brien (born in Co. Clare but a Londoner of long standing) from Irish attack for accepting her Dame of the British Empire honour in 2018, on the grounds that the Irish were active in the Empire, too. Unless you insist that race or ethnicity defines nationality, Dame Edna is at least as British as I am.

That Southern Irish professionals are punching above their demographic weight is clear when you ponder their number in front of the cameras and behind the microphones of the British Broadcasting Corporation, over and above Graham Norton: the late Dave Allen, Des Lynam OBE and his nephew Joe Lynam, Dara O'Briain, Fergal Keane, the impressive ex-convent schoolgirl Orla Guerin MBE, Al Ryan, Angela Scanlon, Declan Harvey and Donnachadh McCarthy. Caroline Lennon from Wicklow who lives in east London played for years an Irish villager in *The Archers*, a fictional emblem of the English heartland. Sinead Keenan from Dublin (married to an *EastEnders* director) is making her career courtesy of the BBC and ITV. The BBC radio presenter Dermot O'Leary is actually first-generation English, having been born in Colchester to where his parents migrated from Ireland; he holds dual British and Irish citizenship and is described in his Wikipedia entry as a "British-Irish" presenter; he is "extremely proud" of his Irish roots, and one hopes that he is proud, too, of his English upbringing; Terry Wogan was an early model for O'Leary. A recent book on writers and the BBC reminds us that even after Radio Éireann was established, Irish writers looked instead to the BBC for opportunities.

There must be dozens of Irish away from the cameras and microphones of the BBC, ITV and Channel Four – producing, directing, scripting, research-assisting. Aisling Bea from Kildare, as well as being a stand-up comedian, writes and stars in Channel 4's comedy drama *This Way Up*; her sister Sinéad (O'Sullivan) Kidao is a costume designer who worked on BBC's *The Pursuit of Love*; naturally they both live in London. Hundreds of Irish work like them at the heart of British culture and help it pump the blood of that culture. Donnachadh McCarthy FRSA was born in Ireland and for a while was a ballet dancer there, before joining the Royal Opera Ballet in Covent Garden. He embedded himself in British culture once he arrived in London in 1986. He lives in a Victorian terrace in Camberwell and has been a Southwark councillor and deputy Chair of the Liberal Democrats. He is a prominent agitator on ecological matters whose CV for the last quarter century reflects an entirely English life. So do those of countless Irish teachers and researchers in the British academy, from colleges and redbricks to Oxbridge itself. At the summit are such eminences in the Humanities as professors Roy Foster FRSL, FBA from Waterford (Hertford College, Oxford), Eamonn Duffy FBA, a "cradle Catholic" (his description) from Dundalk (former President of Magdalene College, Cambridge) and Bernard O'Donoghue FRSL from County Cork (Wadham College, Oxford).

The other disciplines are just as enriched by Irish expertise. Professor Louise Richardson DBE, FRSE, a Catholic from Tramore and whose specialty is terrorism, is the Vice-Chancellor of the University of Oxford and therefore arguably the highest ranking academic in the United Kingdom.[3] It has been said that her leadership at the University of Oxford played an important role in the successful development of a vaccine to combat Covid-19. As it happens, Professor Adrian Hill FRCP from Dublin is Director of the Jenner Institute at the same university and directed the search for the anti-Covid 19 vaccine. Working under Professor Hill at the Institute is Professor Teresa Lambe from Kilcullen, Co. Kildare. Susan Hopkins CBE, who grew up in Kildare and read medicine at Trinity College Dublin, is a specialist in infectious diseases who has been Strategic Response Director for Covid-19 at Public Health England and is a senior lecturer at Imperial College London. In late 2021 she was awarded the Irish government's Presidential Distinguished Service Award, which honours Irish Diaspora members around the world. (It is difficult for me to accept that Irish professionals living and working in Britain inhabit a diaspora.) Meanwhile, Aoife Abbey, 36, from Dublin is an IC unit doctor at University Hospitals Coventry & Warwickshire for whom we can predict a luminous future not only as a doctor but as a writer, author as she is of *Seven Signs of Life: Stories from an Intensive Care Doctor* (2019); she has an autobiographical piece in the *Times* Magazine of May 1, 2020 in which her Irishness tellingly goes unmentioned.

A different kind of professional is the current CEO of British Airways, the nation's carrier. Sean Doyle, who was born and reared in Youghal, Cork, follows Willie Walsh from Dublin as CEO (2005-2011). (Not even the sky is the limit for the Irish in the country of the ancient enemy.) Yet another is the London chef and author Richard Corrigan, born and raised in Ballivor, County Meath, multiple winner of the Great British Menu, and a restaurateur who owns Corrigan's Mayfair, Bentley's Sea Grill in Harrods, Daffodil Mulligan in Islington, and for good measure Virginia Park Lodge in County Cavan. ("Richard Corrigan's Irish Feast," *Times* Magazine, December 7, 2019.) He may think London is led by "a load of donkeys" and the UK by "a bunch of monkeys" (see his Wikipedia entry), but there he is, profitably plying his superb trade in London for decades, too well embedded, I would suggest, for his insults to be anti-British rather than the grievances of an exasperated businessman finding his government boneheaded. Just as successful is Fiona Leahy from Tipperary profiled in a recent *Sunday Telegraph*; she is one of the world's most sought-after event designers, running her agency from London and living joyfully with her boyfriend Alex Antonioni amidst the upmarket Victorian and Edwardian houses of Queen's Park and its "best farmers' market in the UK", as she puts it. Then there is Sir Ciarán Devane who was born in Dublin and graduated from UCD. He was CEO of Macmillan Cancer Support before becoming CEO of the British Council while serving as the non-executive director of NHS England; The Irish Minister for Health, Simon Harris, announced in 2018 that Devane is the first Chair of the Irish Health services (IHS); the British knighted him in 2015 for his services to cancer services.

And I haven't even mentioned the Irish presence in sport in Britain, including, obviously, football and horse-racing, both sports in which there is a unified culture, a continuous, intimate and age-old exchange of talent and management skills. Four of England's Euro 2020 squad are the sons or grandsons of Irish migrants. In the case of horse-racing, trainer JonJo O'Neill at Jackdaws Castle in deepest, darkest England ("in the heart of the [supremely English] Cotswolds", according to his website) and jockey Rachel Blackmore from Tipperary (when she became the first woman jockey to win the Cheltenham Gold Cup there was talk of a damehood for her) can personify the unity. The movement of thoroughbred horseflesh blithely occurs outside the rules of the EU, that bureaucracy that has caused such friction between the two countries during Brexit. Horse-racing is such a mutual Anglo-Irish sport and business that not even the EU can drive that border down the Irish Sea, and nobody in Ireland would dream of doing so. During Brexit negotiations, one *Irish Times* headline ran: "Brexit could decimate Ireland's horse racing industry", but of course it won't: bloodstock is thicker than seawater.

All my names are but tips of an iceberg. The critical mass of Irish presence and talent in Britain makes Irish Anglophobia perversely disconnected from Irish lives in England. And self-harming: whether real or affected, public anti-Britishness shrinks the compass of Irish cultural experience and possibility, and certainly its healthy expression. Why aren't the successful Irish in Great Britain speaking out and saying this? Is something forbidding this?

Four

In 2016, there were 277, 200 people born in the UK living in the Republic where there is a notable historical and ongoing infusion in Ireland of British culture, high, low and middlebrow, via television, radio, cinema, the Internet, newspapers and journals. Often it is a cultural mutuality: as I write, *Normal People*, the BBC TV series from the Irish novel, gets rave reviews and is also being shown on RTÉ. Imported British culture is silently welcomed. Until a few decades ago, British culture was officially discouraged and even denounced as a moral and cultural threat. It was perhaps television transmission that raised the boom because it could not be ambushed by the Republic's film censor as movies were. Before television, surreptitiously tracking the everyday doings of the Brits mingled Irish guilt, pleasure and envy. But Ireland no longer needs to eavesdrop: all it has to do is declare that Britain and Ireland culturally interpenetrate in ways that add to the gaiety of both nations and to neither country's diminishment.

A weekly reminder of this healthy silent mutuality (healthier were it to be openly acknowledged) is on the Irish newsstands each Sunday. The Dublin edition of the London *Sunday Times* rivals that of the *Irish Times* in Southern circulation – 68,500 for the former to 79,000 for the latter (but only 56,500 for the latter's print edition). The Dublin *Sunday Times* is also sold north of the border in disregard of Northern Ireland's being in the UK and therefore eligible to receive the London or Scotland edition; but then, since the columnists and reporters who write for the Dublin edition are both British and Irish, the border between the Republic and Great Britain is equally ignored. Half of the features of the main section of the latest issue at the time of writing are over the names of *Sunday Times* Irish staff writers, while the other half are written by such well-known British figures as Jeremy Clarkson, Wayne Rooney, Niall Ferguson and Peter Conradi. Half of the newspaper's Culture Magazine is written by such Britons as Bryan Appleyard, Jonathan Dean, Max Hastings and John Arlidge. The colour Magazine looks as if it is simply the untouched London edition with thirteen of the fourteen writers British (the other, European) and a four-page feature on V-E Day. In other words, the targeted readership of the *Sunday Times* (Dublin) is all the Irish of the island with a keen investment of interest in what is happening on both sides of the narrow water.

One of the more enlightened of the campaigners to sever

Northern Ireland from the United Kingdom in order to create a constitutionally unified island is Irish High Court Judge Richard Humphreys, author of *Beyond the Border: The Good Friday Agreement and Irish Unity After Brexit* (2018). May I say that in his book he has courteously given me a good deal of elbow room through quotations from my pro-Union articles. Judge Humphreys has written with generosity about unionist sensitivities and believes that a unified Ireland would work only if the British identity of the unionists were sincerely factored in and protected. And that would be helped along, he believes, if Southern Ireland acknowledged the British dimension to its own experience.

But surely Southern Ireland for the sake of its own social health and fidelity to history – and to current reality – would want to acknowledge that dimension with or without Northern Ireland, and moreover should have done so years ago? It shouldn't be the price of annexing Northern Ireland. Judge Humphreys' unavoidable implication is that this dimension has been repressed, and I believe it has. There has been a massive disconnect between the story that Irish politicians and historians tell of the relationship between England and Ireland (usually told in purely political terms and without Scotland and Wales) and the untold truth of cultural history and social reality. The well-intentioned remarks during certain ceremonial occasions about kinship between the two peoples fall comically short of the daily experiences of Irish people on both sides of the Irish Sea. So three short paragraphs on that dimension in a 280-page book suggests to me that even this generous author's heart is not in it.

The book's idea is left unexamined that in a kind of culture reassignment therapy, the Britishness of unionists can be somehow extracted from the UK and grafted on to a united Ireland and "accommodated" therein, while Ireland gaily enjoys its unfettered access to the UK via the media and the Common Travel Area, quietly and officially ignores its own striking British dimension, and asserts instead its ethnic uniqueness. How rich is this? The primacy of Irish ethnic identity – which the campaign for a united Ireland is predicated on – is fine if you wish to ignore the multiculturalism of which Ireland is otherwise seemingly proud, the daily shared experiences that lie below, in and around ethnicity. Ireland has come a long way since a time when commemorating the Great War or welcoming the British Queen would have been unthinkable. Old moulds are being broken. However, there's a marathon distance to go yet, but it requires changes of principle and policy less than it does recognition of the incontrovertible reality of those current and generations-old mutualities that are enacted daily. The Taoiseach Mìcheàl Martin has called for a "re-set" of the UK-EU relationship. It would answer him better to call for a re-set of the UK-Ireland relationship and to do so by making his government's Shared Island Unit the Shared *Islands* Unit.

Five

But are all these Irish in Britain, living, working, sometimes becoming household names, any different from the one million Canadians who live in the United States, where Jim Carrey, Pamela Anderson, Mike Myers, Dan Aykroyd, Malcolm Gladwell, Matthew Perry, William Shatner, Steven Pinker – all Canadian-born – have found fame? No one, after all, is suggesting in Canada's case that because citizens of a smaller English-speaking country gravitate to the neighbouring English-speaking powerhouse to pursue their career that there are any heavy, much less political implications.

But the North American situation is bereft of the ironies that attend the Irish in Britain. And the ironies speak hitherto unspoken volumes. The million Canadians in the United States are 1/38th of the Canadian population; in 2001, one in every six persons born in Ireland lived in Great Britain. This suggests that the term "migrant" is more accurate than "emigrant" when labelling those who cross the water. Britain is an extension of Ireland – even in some sense a colony of the Irish mind. Why does this provoke embarrassment instead of pride back in Ireland? Isn't there national denial at work?

Nor over the decades of Canadian emigration to the U.S. was there anything comparable between the Canadian view of the U.S. that preceded that emigration and Irish emigrants' preconceptions of Great Britain. In *The Forgotten Irish*, Bernard Canavan remarks on the bitter irony in the banishment of boys to Britain – priests in the institutions, he says, would allocate boys to London neighbourhoods: you to Kilburn, you to Cricklewood, you to Camden, and so on). They were being banished to what was regarded as the godless enemy of Ireland! This was surely arrant hypocrisy, or perhaps cognitive dissonance, since Anglophobia was trumped by the brute facts of young Irish work-boots told to step on to British soil. By contrast, educated Irish emigrants simply crossed the Irish Sea without compunction; they weren't deportees and knew better than the Catholic church's nonsense about godlessness and eternal enmity. But unfortunately they have chosen not to speak up.

Furthermore, Canadian emigration to the U.S. involves no political complexity in so far as Canada has no designs on any part of the United States; there is no unfinished constitutional business, no paramilitary campaigns against the U.S. inside its borders. And yet – the Irish keep going to Britain. And they are not turned back at the border; indeed the Common Travel Area means they are treated like returning Britons. This proves that there is a stratum of mutual cultural identity, beneath (or above) the political, a stratum that is thick enough to permit the Irish of all classes to live unmolested in Britain and there flourish (or not) by their own lights. (Though there were, of course, anti-Irish backlashes after bombings, as with the infamous Birmingham bomb, that Sweeney's documentary recalls.)

Nor is there back in Canada a major political party whose primary purpose is to demonise the United States and seek endless redress and concessions from it. And yet tens of thousands of Irish people defy Sinn Féin when they choose to live in Britain, but do not announce their defiance.

Six

Why the silence from both sides of the Irish Sea about Irish relocation to Britain, a silence that encourages the British themselves to keep mum about it? Diarmaid Ferriter writes that the silence was still in force when he left school in 1989, a year in which 70,600 Irish people crossed the water. It is still in force in Britain, and Tony Murray in his April 7, 2014 *Irish Times* article, "The Irish in London in Fact and Fiction", asks: "So, why had Irish writers been so reluctant to represent their own and their compatriots' experiences of migration to London? Why the reticence? Especially given that they were the oldest and, for a long time, the biggest migrant group in the city? Was it shame, indifference, or plain Irish contrariness?" One answer might lie in Ferriter's reminder of how when Richard Mulcahy, Fine Gael leader, dared in 1946 to describe the attractions of Britain to Irish citizens, he was accused by Fianna Fáil of being a recruiting sergeant for a foreign country; the topic was to be regarded as nationally *infra dig* and buried; to discuss it was unpatriotic. (Presumably the patriotism card was to distract from an embarrassment that has still not been addressed.) That code of silence must persevere in vestigial form among the immigrants in Britain themselves, for I read very little from the successful or contented Irish who are established in Britain about their *being* successful or contented. Or if they do talk, they don't seem to be widely reported. That is why the lonely candour of Mary Kenny, Ruth Dudley Edwards, Brendan O'Neill, Kevin Maher and Tony Murray is refreshing and potentially emancipating.

Could it be also that the story of victimhood, a plank of the Sinn Féin platform, is the captivating Irish narrative (in both senses) woven around the complementary strand that Ferriter calls "a single, heroic nationalist narrative of Irish history"? Is to discuss the empirical fact of Irish contentment or success in Britain to be regarded as denying or subverting that double-stranded republican narrative? Is that narrative obligatory, even imperative, and risky to disown?

Think of the trolling Dara Ó Briain gets from the Irish Twitterati even without his adverting to any narrative but simply for being happy and thriving in Britain. "It's always West Brit Season for Irish celebrities working in the United Kingdom," writes Donald Clarke in a January 12, 2019 *Irish Times* article: "All kinds of things can get you called a West Brit these days". Ó Briain has responded wittily to his begrudgers: "By definition, I'm not a West Brit, because I actually live in Britain. I mean, get your insults straight, please". How, then, might the deplorable insult be accurately phrased to identify a highly cultivated man born in Ireland, who speaks fluent Irish, supports the GAA, and who is no doubt patriotic, yet who lives and makes his glittering career in Great Britain? A man, moreover, who is, I wager, more comfortable in his own skin than his detractors.

Yet even O'Briain seems to me to be defensive. One must be sensitive to the baggage involved. First-generation Londoner Sean O'Donovan attended the 2014 Irish Writers in London Summer School and wrote about it in the *Irish Times* of June 2, 2015. It is a touching exercise in the equivocal. On the one hand, he writes of the London-Irish living "abroad" which strikes an odd geographic note. He writes of the "homeless Irish heart" of what he calls the "second-generation Irish". He writes of the London-Irish not wishing to integrate, unlike young Afro-Caribbeans, but instead waging "a fierce battle not to be called British"; he was brought up as an FBI, "Foreign Born Irish with an English accent". He was christened Michael but his mother had him call himself Seán to others to sound more Irish – her choice of separateness over integration. On the other hand, he says, seemingly with cheerful realism and embryonic pride (the cheer and pride are in his rhythm and rhyme): "We grew up in Holloway, not Galway; played on the fields of Peckham Rye, not the fields of Athenry. The education, the environment, the TV and radio we experienced were all different". And he has a fond memory of the 2006 Summer School when one student in the pub afterwards expressed his Irish patriotism yet "was also very emotionally attached to the English football team who were playing Portugal in the World Cup. It was going badly and he was not happy. ... Tony Murray got everyone in that Irish bar in the heart of Holloway to cheer England on for perhaps the first time".

The tiny addendum that England lost on a penalty shoot-out is the joke one uses to cover up one's tears. For there is heartache involved. At the core of O'Donovan's article is the question trying to answer itself: "Is it now possible to remain very proud of being Irish but also begin to acknowledge that growing up in England may possibly have had a positive influence on our lives?" This is a step in a journey towards wholeness, it seems to me. There must be many Irish in Britain who love their lives in Britain; if so, it is a love that dare not speak its name. Literally: O'Donovan's "second-generation Irish" should actually read "first-generation English". In her Wikipedia entry, the comedian and actor Roisin Conaty is referred to as "Irish-English"; her parents met in London, having separately moved to England, and Conaty was born in Camden. On some sites she is referred to as British and I suspect that she is not offended. Daily life in childhood was in Camden, holidays were in Kerry; the difference as she recalls it was between bustling town and remote countryside, not between nationalities or cultures.

If I can risk impertinence, I suspect that Murray's defensiveness reflects the weight of a narrative that proscribes the words and epithets "English" and "British". Proscription prevents self-discovery and liberation from an impersonal and partisan Story (a story of unbridgeable difference and mutual hostility) that is far past its sell-by date. The *Daily Telegraph* economics columnist, Liam Halligan, is first-generation English from an Irish Catholic family. His defence in the April 20, 2019 *Spectator* ("It's not anti-Irish to criticise Leo Varadkar") of his criticism of the Taoiseach for damaging Anglo-Irish relations by his attitude to Brexit, is a remarkable piece of writing. It may have economics at its heart, but it is also heartfelt. The Taoiseach's anti-English approach pained Halligan. "As someone who physically embodies the binding blood and cultural ties between

Britain and Ireland, I'm regularly attacked in the Irish media for having voted to leave". He was supposed to revert to ethnic type and oppose Brexit on the simple grounds of anti-Britishness, not reflect his English upbringing, education, livelihood, and professional economic assessment of the UK's decision to leave the EU. "The fragility of relations between Britain and Ireland is hard-wired into me," Halligan writes. "Having grown up 'London-Irish' in the 1970s and 1980s, all I ever wanted was for the two countries that define my ethnicity to get on". O'Donovan's and Halligan's stories, yet to be fully told, are in their own way as moving as the stories of banished industrial schoolboys.

The proscription applies even more stringently to Irish emigrants in Britain and is aimed at preventing those emigrants from becoming British. The TV presenter Laura Whitmore found out that while the Irish can have successful lives in a tolerant Britain, they must still obey the dictates of the Irish Story. That Story installs the British armed forces as devils incarnate, and so when Whitmore appeared in a British Army podcast, interviewing a female soldier about body issues in a male-dominated occupation, she was tarred and feathered by Irish commentators in the social media for what amounts to treason against Irishness. Her crime was apparently made worse because she followed the interview with a tribute to John Hume who had just died and whose legacy, Whitmore's critics implied, could not permit fraternising with the enemy as Whitmore had just done. ("Laura Whitmore defends decision to appear in British Army podcast after backlash," *Evening Standard*, August 6, 2020.)

This century-old attempt to control the Diaspora is echoed by the Chinese Communist Party's attempt to do likewise in the West and which we rightly deplore. Except, of course, cultural reality and demography suggest that the middle-class and professional-class Irish in Britain are not a Diaspora at all, but simply compatriots across the water. Having just published his third novel, and making his living by talking, Graham Norton, one might think, should be able to articulate the position of the successful Irish in England and set the matter to rights. But he wool-gathers and his language deteriorates when in *The Guardian* of September 26, 2020 he is asked by Alex Clark: "What about the UK, his home for decades now?" His answer seems like displacement activity: "There's a lot of charity shops," he says of English small towns, "I know that. We're raising a lot of money for cancer. But see, that's an odd thing I'll do, where I'll say 'we're' raising a lot of money. And, and so I have *that* thing, because I've lived there since 1984; my career is there, my friends are there, I pay tax there, I vote there. And I work for the British Broadcasting Corporation." Graham, just answer the question. (And identify the repeated "there" and "that country" as "England": that's where your there is and it's your country now!) Instead, he retreats into pretending that in living inside a non-ethnic tribal bubble in England he isn't really living there. "So there is a sense where that's my tribe. Certainly I found a tribe that I can be part of in that country. And so, I've said this before, but it is that thing where I'm in London, I get on the plane, and I'm going home to Ireland. But when I leave here in September, I'm going home to London. And I think you can do that. I don't think we have to be policed that strictly." So who *are* these police? All clarity is evaded as he dances round "that thing" he daren't identify. He cannot simply say: "well, I am as English now as I'm Irish, living as I am the full British life, and that's perfectly understandable and indeed a rather marvellous privilege". That he was speaking from lockdown back in Cork would, of course, have triggered the self-policing more forcefully.

The identity and heritage police include columnists back in Ireland who get very het up if the Irish identity of artists and actors (or anyone) prospering in Great Britain is not loudly proclaimed by the British; indeed, what is crucial to the angry brigade is that the achievers be expressly identified as *not* British. The Irish columnist Ciara O'Loughlin fumed when in 2022 Rachael Blackmore from Tipperary, the first woman jockey to win the Cheltenham Gold Cup, was called British by commentators. (*Irish Independent*, March 24).

O'Loughlin claimed it always happened and put it down to "pure and utter colonial ignorance". But of course if there weren't so many professional Irish living and thriving in Great Britain, treated as honorary Brits by the hospitable English, the mistake would rarely occur. But this indignation usually ignites back in Ireland from those loitering to be offended, far less often from those enjoying British success; but it has a dampening effect on the successful, encouraging them to walk the patriotic line and never to forget Ireland's exceptionalism.

Why does all this matter, and matter to me? When I say that I believe it healthier for Ireland and the Irish to acknowledge and embrace the Irishness of Britain and the Britishness of Ireland, I am being simultaneously self-serving and altruistic. Altruistic because I have a stake in the welfare of Ireland having spent a lifetime in Irish Studies, having lived and loved over the years in Dublin, which I like better than I do Belfast, but cannot see what purpose is served by sequestering (or even denying outright) a huge portion of Irish historical and present reality and the energy and potential for individual and collective fulfilment involved therein. Brexit, alas, and now the Coronavirus, have been exploited by some to reverse in the unspoken name of Little Ireland the amicable potential by the crying up of the differences between the islands. Yet just think of Irish-British relations in the most human, individual and family forms (lives entwined), think of all those living Irish (and dead generations of Irish) in Britain, and the differences shrink to very little.

If I am self-serving, it is because as a Northern Irishman who regards himself as both Irish and irrevocably British, I am offended by the hypocrisy of a political campaign to rescind my Britishness while the Republic of Ireland represses its own British dimension, at home and over the water. Let the Republic do its psychic work and unionists will do theirs, which involves accepting their Irish differences from the mainland British.

I suspect, in fact, that many Southern Irish would be relieved by being able to acknowledge openly, even celebrate, Britain and Ireland's intimate relations. But the Irish are held to ransom by state and Sinn Féin republicanism. A national superego forbids such acknowledgement, much less celebration. But historical and current reality should not be the captive of a political position. Fianna Fáil Senator Mark Daly wants to convene a New Ireland Forum 2 in order to dispel unionist fears of the inevitable united Ireland; I suggest the Forum instead explore the intimate mutual relations between Ireland and Britain, relations which are no threat to Irish patriotism but are the proper starting-point for a search for final peace on these islands. Such a frank audit, with no one afraid of betraying shoneenism, would liberate energies and dynamics heretofore under taboo and embargo. Think of the diversity of occupation, career and talent that could form the panels and interviewees of such a forum!

Seven

We have to accept, though, that recent cultural developments have supervened to qualify the hope for candour about Irish-British relations. Brendan O'Neill, the editor of *Spiked*, has written about this in one of the most provocative pieces I have yet read on the Irish in Britain: "Bad Immigrants" (September 28, 2018). Since he lives in England I assume he could provide case-studies to illustrate his claims. In any event, as a stimulating contrarian, he is refreshingly devoid of defensiveness, guilt, embarrassment, shame, or equivocation when writing as a first-generation Englishman.

During what he calls the second Irish exodus in the second half of the twentieth century (the first was the era of Sweeney's subjects), O'Neill's parents left "the unforgiving boglands of the west of Ireland as teenagers in 1968 and arrived in a Swinging London that perplexed them as much as it thrilled them". Even at that time, Irish immigrants on certain rungs of the social ladder could be regarded as bad immigrants for not fitting in, while being reminded one way or the other that they could never fit in because they were disliked.

Yet O'Neill's parents surmounted all obstacles and never pleaded the poor mouth; they were simply newcomers who wished to succeed. The Irish migrants of the third wave arrived from the 1980s during an economically bleak period in the Republic, and many of them were different from their predecessors in being highly educated: by 1989, 30% of college graduates left Ireland. These formed the early NIPPLE cohort. Many flourished just as tensions between Ireland and Britain because of the Troubles were easing. "And yet here is the curious thing," writes O'Neill, "the new promise of accelerated assimilation, the removal of such blocks to assimilation as anti-Catholicism and fear of Irish republicanism, did not lead to a waning of Irish identity, but to the opposite - it coincided with an explosion of new and ever-more self-conscious and separatist expressions of Irish identitarianism in Britain". Something widespread is at work, including identity politics and the philosophy of multiculturalism. This, says O'Neill, has actively discouraged the Irish, and all the other hyphenated identities in Britain, from integrating in the way, and to the extent, that O'Neill's parents did.

O'Neill sees the active encouragement of difference, the cultivation and institutionalisation of diversity, the discouragement of integration – all at the expense of social cohesion, even coherence – as deplorable, leading to the emergence of "coexisting lifestyles – that is, of communal distinction". Western European societies "have abandoned the social project of assimilation" (itself now a taboo word) and have created the spectre "of socially sanctioned separateness" where immigrants are encouraged to think of themselves as victimised and hostile to their host nation. In the Irish case, O'Neill alleges, the new sense of separatism has taken on vivid expressions of Irish nationalism as the Irish in Britain have self-racialised during "the new Irish identitarianism" – being anti-British; Gaelicising their names and their children's names; assuming by historical proxy the status of victim, when they themselves are anything but.

O'Neill's article was a response to a hostile piece in the *Guardian* that accused him of being a bad Irish immigrant because, unlike the bad immigrants of the past who wouldn't integrate, O'Neill *wishes* to integrate and "wants to feel part of [my host nation], in a real, grown-up way". The subtitle of his article is "I am Irish but I want to be British – is that bad?" So not only is the former encouragement by the host country to assimilate held to be right-wing, but the immigrants' voluntary *wish* to assimilate and embrace the values of their adopted home is just as bad, according to those who are not in any shape or form victims, such as *Guardian* columnists.

If O'Neill is correct about the younger Irish professionals in Britain, then a call for the Irish in Britain to acknowledge the Britishness of their lives, and the Irish in the Republic to acknowledge the British dimension of their own Irish lives, might fall on deaf ears on both sides of the Irish Sea. Nationalism is stronger in the Republic than it has been for decades and has reinforced the northern republican push for a united Ireland. If only those in the Republic could see that the momentous and oddly unremarked Common Travel Area (allowing free movement to and fro between two countries with a history of tension) remains an incipient centrifugal force for expansion, a possible blueprint and inspiration for a structural expression of British-Irish relations. An ideal polity would reflect intimate Irish-British relations. Anyway, deaf ears will not alter one whit the incontrovertible and potent reality of the Irish in Britain and cultural Britain among the Irish. There is little cultural and social rationale for the political campaign to separate Northern Ireland (with its huge component of Britishness) from the British Isles in order to create a larger Republic of Ireland. For that Republic will be (as far as the eye can see) in many ways culturally indistinct from the rest of the United Kingdom; distinct by assertion but in fact part of the same supranational cultural and social entity that is the British Isles.

In the New York St Patrick's Day parade in 2019 the leader of Sinn Féin, Mary Lou McDonald, helped hold up a large banner reading ENGLAND GET OUT OF IRELAND.[4] It would be laughable if it weren't such a grim assault by an arthritic ideology on social reality. (2021/2023)

1   "Republic: Problem or Solution", *Index on Censorship*, vol. 22, 8–9 (1993).
2   He tells his story in his Brian Lenihan Memorial Lecture, Sidney Sussex College, Cambridge, September 14, 2023. Besides being a Commander of the British Empire, he is a Knight of Justice of the Order of St John, suggesting a delicate balance of honours.
3   In the summer of 2023, Professor Richardson was appointed to chair an Irish government forum on Irish security policy and neutrality. President Higgins in a remark thought by some to question her objectivity in the matter referred in distaste to her "very large letter DBE".
4   In late August 2023, the Irish language hip-hop band Kneecap from Belfast unveiled a republican mural in the west of the city captioned England Get Out of Ireland. A film about the republican band is financed by the British Film Institute with National Lottery funds. Ireland's relationship with Britain is entangled in unacknowledged ironies.

A debate on Irish unity?
Some items for the agenda

The calls from Irish nationalist politicians and commentators for a border referendum, or for the Irish government to prepare for the referendum – by which is meant, preparation for the expected Yes vote and after – have grown clamorous of late. Sinn Féin's age-old uninflected chant about unification (which by definition requires no expatiation, defence or debate), has been recently harmonised, as it were, by the "Ireland's Future" organisation which lends social and academic heft to the campaign for a united Ireland. And also by the Irish Seanad's recent public consultation "On the constitutional future of the island of Ireland" and whose report, I think it's fair to say, is unlikely to conclude that unification of the island and total constitutional separation of all thirty-two counties from the United Kingdom, is not on the cards. By comparison, Micheál Martin's Shared Island Unit is a cautious and patient affair, though in its case, too, "sharing" aspires to mean – let's be honest – "getting the North" (to use Yeats's phrase) but by means of a ten-year plan of friendly interpenetration and then friendly persuasion. These are, respectively, the short game and the long game.

Currently the effort is almost entirely unilateral, which has not staunched the one-way flow. This reflects the relatively simple forcefulness that most Irish republicans – by whom I mean Irish nationalists actively in pursuit of a united Ireland severed from the

UK – seem to regard the united Ireland campaign as requiring. There is an obliviousness that is the campaign's hallmark. We know that Sinn Féin expect merely to outpoll and then swamp unionists. They despise unionists, are deaf to their concerns, and in any case their ideology compels them never to deign to debate or convince their sworn enemies; their century-old mandate is merely to cancel unionism. Payback time in their eyes will be brief and decisive.

Even the political historians think it a one-way railroad on which the locomotive is already in motion. In his review essay on Brendan O'Leary's new book, *Making Sense of a United Ireland*, Andy Pollak confesses himself a convert to O'Leary's irreversible direction of travel and the simple requirement of 50+1% in a border referendum.[1] The enduring teleology of Irish republicanism is a wondrously freeing thing: once embraced, it liberates you from the obligations of debate into the fascinating world of mere detailed implementation with all the conceptual, even ludic allure (in words) of those video games in which you build cities and countries from scratch. You get to ponder tasty choices: will the united Ireland be a federal or a unitary state? Who will take on the loyalists – the Irish state or the IRA? O'Leary's book is congested with such meticulous scenarios, as is Richard Humphrey's *Beyond the Border* (2018). Reading such books as a unionist is like being present at one's own elaborate funeral.

But beyond the detailed projections, the broad confident, arational premises of nationalism remain and are not always pretty. It should be notorious by now that the Social Democratic and Labour Party leader Colum Eastwood greeted the recent Northern Ireland census returns as "a seminal moment" in recent Irish history because more citizens declared themselves as Catholics than as Protestants. He hoped that his fellow Catholics could "breathe a sigh of relief". It is as though the "oppressive state which engrained discrimination against a Catholic minority" could have returned like a revenant any time up to the day the census returns were released. So all along it had been down to how many dig with whichever foot. Now, as other nationalist leaders likewise proclaimed, constitutional change is greenlit. Quite simple really: the micks have it, the prods done for.

The very day I read the SDLP statement, I happened to read Sean O'Casey's letter to Paul Shyre, the American producer and playwright, defending the realism of events in *Cock-a-Doodle-Dandy*. He referenced the Killaloe case, its months' long aftermath unfolding as he wrote.

In 1958, three Protestant evangelists in the Co. Clare village where water-skiing was introduced to Ireland that same year, ignored the precaution of practising their religion discreetly in the South. O'Casey related to Shyre what happened, which was corroborated by O'Casey's editor, Prof. David Krause. As O'Casey tells it, a violent little crowd gathered and the Gardai advised the evangelists to move on. They obeyed but on their way to their car the crowd attacked with fists and sticks. When charges were lodged against the assailants, the case against three Catholic farmers was dismissed by the District Justice. Here's the kicker: the DJ said the evangelists deserved their beating and that, in any case, "religion is above the courts".

Adds O'Casey: "Not the evangelists' religion, of course, but the religion of the assailants". The police, the law, the Catholic Church in a common sectarian pursuit: was this not engrained and systemic discrimination, and did it not demonstrate a covenant between Catholic Church and Irish State enshrined in the 1937 Irish Constitution?

Am I dredging up a past within living memory (I was in grammar school when the incident in Killaloe happened) that I hope southerners will find embarrassing? Yes. For I implore the South not to pursue the unity campaign at this time unless it is prepared to deplore, as it requires the North to do, elements of its own nature and tracts of its own history while re-identifying the hitherto blameless, even heroic, as wrongdoers. This is necessary work that has not yet begun in the Republic: if any preparation be needed, it involves this project of national introspection.

A campaign for unity founded on the premise of historical oppression and state failure in Northern Ireland and sunny equity and state success in the Irish Free State and Irish Republic, and founded, too, on the premise of only one constitutional solution to our problems on the island, will not fly. If the unification issue really spills into the unprepared public sphere, we will all relive the nightmare of history from which James Joyce said we were trying to awake.

Yet the unification campaign is founded precisely on Irish history and its alleged imperatives. I seem to recall one indefatigable board member of "Ireland's Future" defining unification as the completing of the 1916 Project. So I'm afraid any unification debate is going to draw in the historians, if only to explain to us what the 1916 Project is perceived to have been if not Pearse's vision of a sovereign Catholic, Gaelic, myth-driven, mystical, non-capitalist, peasant collectivism with a warrior caste, or else Connolly's vision of a worker's republic.

Inevitably, any confirmed unionists who become involved in planning a new Ireland will bring up the past fate of Protestants over the border. One southern Protestant historian has pre-emptively (and unconvincingly) assured northern Protestants that the alarming collapse in the Protestant population since 1922 (from roughly 10% to 3% before a slight recovery to 4%) has had diverse causes, and that systemic discrimination was not among them. Even the Ne Temere decree affecting mixed marriages was not crucial in his eyes, though a prominent Ulster psychiatrist, quoting Hubert Butler along the way, sees the decree as indeed the chief culprit.[2] That is the premiss also of the splendidly directed and acted 1999 RTE-BBC film, *A Love Divided*, a dramatisation of the 1957 Catholic boycott of Protestant businesses in Fethard-on-Sea (Wexford) The boycott was organised by the local priest after a Protestant wife, renouncing the pledge she signed when she married to bring her children up Catholic, fled with her children to Scotland in order to prevent their enforced enrolment in the local Catholic school. The script is sympathetic to husband and wife and unsympathetic to the priest;

Rome is portrayed as guided by realpolitik which provides the cynical resolution,

The southern Protestant historian's depiction of his co-religionists who didn't leave the Free State but stuck it out, staying "at home", keeping their heads down and practising their religion in "privacy", makes sad and embarrassing reading; Protestants suffered, he claims, only "low-level slights and intimidation" and "didn't do badly". In *A Love Divided*, the local Protestant minister refuses to help his parishioner, telling her that "the prevailing wisdom is that we [Protestants] keep our head down and our mouths shut". If the current unity campaign actually became a real and serious debate, I suspect some buried resentment among southern Protestants would disinter itself. An early signal of that resentment was, of course, expressed by W.B. Yeats in 1925 when he told the Irish Senate, about to ratify the bill to outlaw divorce, that this was an insult to Protestants. Rebuked from the chair for his apparent bitterness, he replied "We shall be all much bitterer before we are finished with this question". I think the Tánaiste glimpsed the possible updating of this warning when he addressed the recent Dublin unity gathering.

It is all far too soon and too headstrong. Southerners are being led into this by a small number of public activists and propagandists, lending the kind of respectability that Sinn Féin cannot enjoy at present, because they still celebrate those who carried out terrorist atrocities for thirty years.[3] Senator Daly and Prof. Colin Harvey are in a hurry. Southerners would be wise to fall sensibly back and reflect on what may imminently lie in wait.

In Northern Ireland there will be a deepening polarisation between nationalists and unionists, Catholics and Protestants. Rallies, meetings, "debates" in the highly territorial public sphere will provoke protests and probably worse since unhealed wounds heighten sensitivities and inflame feelings. The Alliance Party, growing in numbers of those voters who want to get on with life at a level below the constitutional and beyond the religious, solving issues that are not political at the national identity level, will implode. Party members will be pressed to declare themselves on the very issue whose avoidance was the party's *raison d'etre*. In a febrile constitutional scrummage, the centre cannot hold. Pro-Union party members will desert and probably head for the UUP. A crucial time-sensitive work in progress – making a non-sectarian Northern Ireland work which I have always thought a prerequisite to any reasonable talk of a united Ireland – will be cancelled overnight.

Other unforeseen fractures will appear in Southern society, too, were the "debate" to move from rhetoric to reality. Has anyone in the South apart from Justice Richard Humphreys considered at length what concessions are to be made to beguile unionists? (And his proposed concessions, though generous under the circumstances of the current Republic, fail completely to assure me.) On the question of a new flag. Of a new national anthem. Of the official role of Ulster Scots dialect in public sector life. Of unionist symbols to be incorporated into the Southern public sphere. Of the future status of the Catholic Church in 90% of the South's primary schools. Of the bureaucratic compulsion of the Irish language. Not to speak of representation in an entirely new police force. Dubliner Vincent Keaveny, lately Lord Mayor of London, pondered the intimacy of Ireland and England in his Brian Lenihan Memorial Lecture at Cambridge University in September 2023. Thinking of what changes Republic of Ireland citizens would entertain to accommodate northern unionists, he admitted that support for a united Ireland drops significantly if a new anthem or a new flag is the cost to be paid. One-way street thinking still prevails.

Do unity campaigners imagine the Republic will reinvent itself in happy unanimity? If hard-line republicans are driving the campaign, there will be civic war as the object of Irish citizenship is contested. Already, the question of how to speak publicly of IRA bombings and shootings has divided southerners after Mary Lou McDonald saw no comparison, moral or otherwise, between contemporary gangland murders (bad) and IRA paramilitary killings unsanctioned by the Irish state (justified). How to narrate the IRA terror campaign, 1970–1994, into the history books will be an incensing challenge.

Or do campaigners think instead that almost a million unionists will quietly assimilate to the Republic as it is and so pre-empt the need for any Southern soul-searching?

In fact, it would be necessary to strip out all extant and residual anti-British, anti-Protestant and anti-unionist political and cultural manifestations so that no public spaces would make unionists feel unsafe or uncomfortable: this is the new human rights landscape of western liberal societies. (And human rights advocates and lawyers will be dancing attendance.) The Republic prides itself in being a progressive liberal society; it would have to prove it in its biggest test ever. And would it be recognisable thereafter if it did? How many citizens welcome sea-changes to a society in which they're on the whole content? And perhaps need to face higher taxes to pay for the sea-change?

The national Story would have to be re-told. Why? Because, as the historian Jeff Fynn-Paul reminded us in his recent *Spectator* essay on the new and darker Story of the discovery and settlement of North America that is vying with the familiar Story for dominance, "It is times like these that we realise the stories we tell ourselves — about our history in particular — are of fundamental importance to the direction our societies take. The shift from Weimar Republic to Nazi Germany was accomplished, first and foremost, by a shift in who controlled the national narrative. Ditto with the shift to Communism in eastern Europe, as so movingly chronicled by the late Tony Judt in his book *Postwar*." In the Irish case, the national Story would need to be retold in order to avoid the absurdity of unionists being "invited" to unite with a country in whose Story they (or the British as a whole) are the villains.[4]

So content and perspectives offensive to pro-British and pro-Union sensibilities would have to be removed. New school textbooks would need to be written to promote parity of esteem and a balance between unionist and nationalist values, heroes and icons. Easter 1916 and the War of Independence could no longer be the "onlie begetters" of a unified island, but merely significant, contested partisan contributions. In *Unherd* recently (November 21), Norma Costello wrote of the Republic: "This is a nation with a national anthem entitled 'The Soldier's Song'. Our war for independence [against the British] is the most deified part of our history books." Will the "deified" or venerated be voluntarily reduced to the prosaic and scrutinizable? "Amhrán na bhFiann" ("The Soldier's Song") by Kearney and Heeney would have to go.

Irish participation in the Great War and Ulster's in the Battle of the Somme and Northern Ireland's industrial contribution to the struggle against Germany in the Second World War (the same Germany that Irish republicans approached for help in both wars) would demand equality in the telling and the valuation. Southerners whose forebears over centuries served in the British army and navy might support this project of redress, not least those whose grandfathers and great-grandfathers faced obloquy and disgrace when they returned to the Irish counties at wars' ends; but this would be divisive.

Then there is the question of the Republic's official refusal to take sides in times of war, which is in stark contrast to the unionist fidelity to Britain's military record. The former leader of the Ulster Unionist party, Steve Aitken, has claimed that in the unlikely event of a united Ireland, unionists would demand the end of Irish neutrality.[5] Indeed, with the expansion of NATO in response to Russian aggression in Ukraine, and plans for countries in the EU to achieve a state of military readiness, the Republic is already coming under pressure inside and outside its borders to abandon its strict neutrality which in any case may have been originally embraced as a way of separating itself from one more British characteristic.

Besides, Irish neutrality in terms of home defence is a proxy evasion. In an article, Ian Paisley Jr MP reminds us that "RAF aircraft are called upon to help defend Irish airspace in an emergency. An

Irish government-appointed Commission on the Defence Forces said the Republic of Ireland 'has no air defence capability of any significance'... An assault on the Republic or an attempt to sabotage vital communication infrastructure such as sub-sea cables could adversely impact NI." (*News Letter*, July 5, 2023). And in the larger theatre of war, as Conor Gallagher puts it, "Nato protects Ireland without the need for any potentially divisive [Irish] national debate" (*Unherd*, Octber 27, 2023). But that debate would have to occur if unification became a serious prospect. Gallagher's title is "The Myth of Irish Neutrality" and this myth, for which he offers copious examples from recent history, would have to be dragged into public view and either accepted as true or invalidated by a firm new commitment to neutrality. (In all probability, a reaffirmed neutrality would not survive a debate about the real world and the emerging new world order.) This part of the national Story clearly badly needs updating.

Beyond military intervention, the Republic is certainly not impartial in international crises. After the Hamas massacre of Jews at the Re'im music festival in October 2023 and Israel's military response, the Irish government maintained its openly acknowledged anti-Israel, pro-Palestine policy, the Irish President, Taoiseach and commentators berating Israel. In South Korea soon after the massacre, speaking to the Irish media, Leo Varadkar said Israel wouldn't consider Ireland a close friend or ally "because we do take a different position than most western countries on Palestine" (*Irish Independent*, November 3, 2023). "We" includes the Irish political parties in the Republic including, especially, Sinn Féin.

The Republic's anti-Israel foreign policy is repugnant to unionists who have been solidly pro-Israel for some time. This is an issue between nationalists and unionists because it has its deep and separate cultural roots, involving among other things the very different attitude to Jews in modern Irish Catholicism (with its foreign policy legacy) and Irish Protestantism, two interpretive traditions of Christianity which inform the two cultures beyond the boundaries of religion. Any unification debate would have to confront this divide which, at the moment of writing, is in crisis beyond Ireland and threatens the West. An all-island debate with foreign policy on the agenda might reveal that the Republic's policy of military neutrality and diplomatic partisanship in the troubled Middle East theatre might not, in fact, be as representative of Southern citizens as assumed; in that debate, any restraints on hitherto hidden dissent would be lifted.

Any debate or convention would also have on its agenda the humble poppy. This yearly buttonhole adornment is a potent symbol of loyalty to, and reverence for, British military sacrifice since, and especially including the Great War. Northern nationalists increasingly show their contempt for the poppy, and it is doubtful if any nationalist could plumb the depth of emotion unionists invest in the cause the flower represents. However, in any unhindered public discussion of the matter, a buried respect for commemoration of the sacrifices of the Great War might surface in the South, especially among the descendants of the tens of thousands of Catholic Irish who fought in that war, and many British wars before it; the public and official orthodoxy in the Republic might well be tested.

And what is to be done about the anti-colonialism that pervades Irish attitudes to the past and present and drives foreign policy? Or about the inherited colonialism of unionism - inherited in personal history from the Ulster Plantation and in shared history with the rest of the United Kingdom? At the time of writing, there is no evidence that a unionist take on the past is reversing itself into the national self-loathing that is occurring among the woke progressives of the English-speaking world. The Truth and Reconciliation task is going to be daunting.

And of course, Bunreacht Na hÉireann would have to be radically revised as an Irish-British, nationalist-unionist constitutional hybrid stripped of any embedded veneration for a way of life inimical to unionists.

Unless campaigners think that unionists will just have to subscribe to the winner's account of the past in classrooms and on government websites? Those implementing moves towards unification would have to quickly acquire a knowledge of northern unionism they simply do not have, much less a jot of sympathy. Certainly they have misread unionism up to now. They appear to believe that unionists who voted Remain in the Brexit referendum were indirectly voting for a united Ireland. They fail to understand that no amount of betrayal by British governments induces many unionists to want to leave the UK.

So why not start now by engaging with all the recent arguments for retention of the Union made by educated unionists, a proper engagement that has never taken place. Pollak quotes O'Leary on the culture of contempt among Ulster Protestants towards Irish Catholics. I certainly remember it in the past, though the contempt was really a pre-empting fear. But I have always thought the refusal of nationalists to engage with responsible unionism its own species of contempt. I wanted to write "intellectual unionism" but I know nationalists disbelieve such a thing exists. Nor do they really believe that there is a genuine unionist culture, but only a loyalist subculture of defiance and negation, of bonfires, semi-secret organisations, Orange parades and flags. There is of course a unionist culture - it is British culture of which unionist culture is a regional inflection or dialect but which is available in large measure to unionists as it is to those many thousands of southern Irish living in Britain (and even to those living in the twenty-six counties).

As part of the national culture, even the Irish literary canon would need to be radically revised, with all those distinguished writers thought to be "really" English needing to be incorporated, thus changing the canon in the way T.S. Eliot envisaged. The Irish canon, shaped (like Irish literary criticism) by the Irish Literary Revival, could no longer be one that sits nicely enough with the national story of oppression of the peasantry; resistance by the heroic; victory or continuing undaunted struggle. One in which Shaw, Wilde, C.S. Lewis, Forrest Reid, Joyce Cary and others, are anomalously Irish, in which the numerous Irish women writers contemporary with, but unconnected to, the Irish Revival and its cultural nationalism and who set their work on either side of the Irish Sea, have been ignored. Eliot once explained figuratively how a major new work of literature changes the canon by likening the work to a new passenger entering an elevator, causing the occupants to shuffle in space to accommodate the newcomer. Imagine this social and political as well as literary outcome on an industrial scale in the twenty-six counties. Thus far, those unificationists generous enough to suggest "accommodating" the Britishness of unionists in a united Ireland, seem to imagine an eventuality that requires little or no repositioning of those already in the 26-county elevator.

Yet all of the above has had to be done in Canada, for example, to reconcile French and English and now Indigenous and settler despite the fact that they all share a significant Canadianness in common, as all of us in Ireland share an Irishness, often willingly and happily. New constitutions, acts and laws had to be framed, new perspectives and historical interpretations to be accepted. But is the Irish national consciousness even close to a place where it would accept such fundamental concessions, such a radical re-telling of the Irish Story and reorganisation of Southern society?

In short: who are the chief drivers of the unity campaign? If they are hard-line republicans, there will be division sown in the 26 counties.

Then there are the established dynamics of reconciliation and unification movements elsewhere. There would have to be apologies from the South for systemic discrimination and the excesses of nationalism including pro-IRA sentiments and support if it wishes to secure unionist apologies for their own past sectarianism and paramilitarism, though in his Nobel acceptance speech, David Trimble began such an apology. There would probably be calls for reparations from various interest groups, as there have been in Canada.

Are those calling for a unification debate, border poll and referendum campaign, and who are determined to dismantle Northern Ireland, aware of all this? Do they care? And just when it seemed, certainly before Brexit (which brains bigger than mine are trying to solve), that Catholics and Protestants were coming together in a shared home place, when those of a Catholic or nationalist background could even take the lion's share of the capital city's administering. And the strong statistical remnants of that recent healthy confluence are there in the census returns if Colum Eastwood had looked beyond Protestant and Catholic. Who knows where this may have led in a generation once Northern Ireland was sincerely made to work and unionists no longer felt besieged?

Do Southern unificationists realise that the current as well as past realities of Irish society will come under the lamp? If those campaigning for a united Ireland imagine unionists require only satisfactory answers to questions posed by republicans, they are mistaken.

What intentions are there in the South to acknowledge and reinforce the third, east-west strand of the Good Friday Agreement by giving institutional body to the reality of the daily gravitational pull of British society on Irish lives, the innumerable "British characteristics" of Southern society? How can those demanding a unified island separate from the UK explain away the fact that London is the cultural capital of all of Ireland? (The latest, quite unnecessary exhibit A: Louis Walsh's advice that broadcaster and impressionist Doireann Garrihy get out of Ireland and hotfoot it to the UK "because she's made for bigger things".) How will they respond to the claim that a new Ireland is possible only if there is a new archipelago after the Republic fully acknowledges its inextricable, mutually profitable and mutually enriching connections with the neighbouring island?

It would have to be explained how the demonstrable extent of the Britishness of Irish culture and the intimacy of Irish-English social relations (facilitated by the generous Common Travel Area, whereby hundreds of thousands of southern Irish happily live, work and vote in the UK), could possibly justify a destabilising of the archipelago in order to found a 32-county republic. A republic, moreover, that cannot possibly be sovereign because it is a loyal EU state and will still be economically and culturally inter-dependent with the Great Britain it purports to be severing itself from.

Craig Raine's visiting Martian on his postcards home would likely think the obvious solution would be the Republic's acknowledgment of the peculiar deficits of Irish autonomy, its overdue reconciliation with the neighbouring island it cannot live without (and regards with mingled envy, prurience, distaste and need), and the realism of a renewed eastward direction of travel. Pollak quotes O'Leary on his unification scheme: "Our plan must expansively accommodate the prospective losers. But not too much. The plan must be sufficiently credible that Southerners will not fear for the stability of their hard-won constitutional republic." This is a condescending example of having one's cake and eating it. And you don't get to control the genie once it's out of the bottle: O'Leary's titular "making sense" as interpreting is one thing; "making sense" as making it all sensible and thus feasible is quite another. The Republic was certainly hard-won over many, many decades. But remember that Northern Ireland had to be hard-defended during an internal siege during thirty recent years of terrorist onslaught.

If we don't pull back from this premature and disruptive campaign, I'm tempted to put a menacing traditional Chinese spin on Bob Dylan's line in his great dark lament, "Mississippi": "Things should start to get interesting right about now". I hope Southern onlookers are also listening. (2022/2023)

1   *Dublin Review of Books* 149, November 2022.

2   So too, does Robin Bury in his book *Buried Lives: The Protestants of Southern Ireland* (2017), p. 120. The decree of 1907 under Pope Pius X (which was not superseded until 1970) required a mixed marriage (Catholic and non-Catholic) to be witnessed by a priest; the couple were to give a written guarantee that children were to be brought up in the Roman Catholic faith.

3   In September 2023, Bono of U2 chipped in, assuring Channel 4 News that Northern Ireland and the Republic were now dating, with a falling in love and marriage on the cards pretty soon. (Reported in the *Irish Times*, September 29.) Actually, if you wanted to reach for this particular metaphor, then the relentless harrying of northern unionists by unificationists could be likened to sexual harassment of those whose "No" is to be smothered in the unwanted embrace. Marriage triumphs in *A Love Divided* because real love inspired it; thus far the unification campaign has shown no realpolitik nor even addressed the emotive powers that must be reconciled.

4   Speaking of safe public spaces and the Story: a musician was told by the manager of the Crown Bar in Wexford that there was to be no repeat of the (wildly popular) Irish rebel songs he sang during his set, as they had offended several people. A social media storm ensued and Joe Brolly, well-known broadcaster and barrister, weighed in against the ban. The Bar owners overrode the manager and apologised, welcoming the singing of rebel songs. The musician subsequently was offered gigs in London, Belfast and Europe. A Canary Island Irish pub owner invited him to come and play the "REAL Irish Music". *Irish Independent*, November 14, 2023. The complainants could have been English tourists, Northern Irish unionists or sensitive Southerners; in any case, expect more such incidents should any real debate on Irish unification begin. (2023)

5   https://www.newsletter.co.uk/news/defence/ex-nuclear-submarine-commander-dubs-irish-government-freeloaders-over-lack-of-military-power-and-dependence-on-uk-and-nato-4143705

Doorstep Colonialism

Unionist hackles rose when Richard Neal, in Northern Ireland as part of a congressional delegation, professed the American desire to enable "the planter and the Gael to live together".[1] Yet as an east Belfastman of presumably Ulster Scots ancestry, I never thought the term "planter" derogatory. Back in 1975 I published an essay in the *Canadian Journal of Irish Studies* called "The Landscape of Planter and Gael in the Poetry of John Hewitt and John Montague", reprinted in my book *Colonial Consequences: Essays in Irish Literature and Culture* (1991).

My essay was inspired by the tour the poets Hewitt and Montague made around Northern Ireland in the late 1960s on the eve of the Troubles, sponsored by the Northern Ireland Arts Council. I don't recall any objections to the tour's title, "The Planter and the Gael", and at that time "planter" may even have been a compliment. Hewitt, a Belfastman, loved the glens of County Antrim, which like County Down was not part of the Ulster Plantation. Yet he was happy to embody and sing the virtues and vices of the planter, just as Montague, a lapsed Catholic born in Brooklyn, was happy to be the Paris-based Gael in his life and poetry.

A.T.Q. Stewart reminded us in *The Narrow Ground: Roots of Conflict in Ulster* (1977), of "the continuous natural influx of Scottish settlers" into Ulster before and after the organised Plantation of the 17th century. Planters came to mean any Dissenter

Protestants in Ulster, and the twin terms, Planter and Gael, were recruited to signify the cultural cleft in Ulster life between native and settler and which later in the 1970s was celebrated as the Two Traditions.

Yet words and phrases carry changing meanings and value judgements over time and by context. It's unlikely that Neal, a professed Irish republican in politics, meant "planter" as an honorific though perhaps he did. However, the other relevant context besides American support for Irish nationalism is the ongoing project in the U.S. in schools and universities to Decolonise history and society. Neal's term "planter" now has the Decolonisation revolution over its shoulder. This revolution is under way in other parts of the English-speaking world, including the UK, but is most advanced in New Zealand, Canada and Australia, the old "white Dominions".

My academic colleagues in British Columbia now refer to themselves as "settler scholars". In their email signatures they admit they are teaching on "unceded" Indigenous territory. They are not just descendants of colonial planters, they publicly confess, but are in a real sense planters themselves, and that is something for which they therefore must apologise and atone, while of course declining, like all the growing number of self-confessed (indeed, eagerly self-professed) anti-colonialists in British Columbia, to absent themselves from the unceded ground their desk sits on.

The prestigious Royal British Columbia Museum (RBCM) in the province's capital, Victoria, has closed its doors, having emptied its galleries of "colonial" displays as part of its Decolonisation & Indigenisation Project, one of the action programmes called for by the federal Truth & Reconciliation Commission (2015). When it reopens, there will be a radically new interpretation and presentation of British Columbia history, centring on Indigenous culture.

The native galleries in the museum, that were already significant and impressively displayed, with the extraordinary carved masks of the Kwakiutl and other first nations (Indian tribes, in American usage), could certainly be augmented and given a richer Indigenous cultural context. But it is equally certain that the extraordinary British "discovery" (for Europeans), exploration, natural history, settlement and development of the vast province will be cut down in size and re-cast in a negative light. Already much-loved galleries, such as a three-dimensional Ulster Folk Museum-type multi-media depiction of early Victoria, have been denigrated by curators and dismantled. When the museum reopens, the "Royal" in its name will almost certainly be gone.[2]

Publicly-funded museum administrators in English-speaking countries nowadays seem to wish to make the bulk of their traditional visitors feel bad about their own culture. They have taken it upon themselves less to entertain, educate, and engender a sense of wonder than to display for the visitors the sins of their ancestors. They have become our unelected and often unqualified culture-givers and historical interpreters, along with art gallery owners and boards of non-profit organisations such as Oxfam and the National Trust. (In the case of museums, the qualified curators have seemingly little say in the unfolding agenda.)

In a recent article (May 14), *News Letter* editor Ben Lowry identified six events or factors that have wounded Ulster unionism. His fourth is the culture war. He is thinking of the progressive liberalism that has challenged traditional unionism. But in the form of cancel culture, the war is now coming closer to Northern Ireland from the rest of the English-speaking world. It is brewing, for example, among local (though not necessarily locally-educated) museum curators.

At a recent Queen's University-Ulster Museum conference, the Head of Curatorial at NI museums declared "the imperative to decolonise [our] collections, sites, structures and activities. ... We absolutely should interrogate the British Empire and its legacy". Where did this imperative come from? She is appalled by "the spectre of colonial violence and injustice" (she doesn't say where, exactly) and believes that the museums' task is to tackle racism through Decolonisation. Decolonisation includes removing certain objects from public view, presumably out of shame. Whence the authority or consensus for this?

The return of artifacts to their indigenous home is a sensitive and legitimate subject for museums, of course. But any return of objects to their faraway cultures of origin, or removal into storage, is inevitably accompanied by unanimous denunciation of Britain and its colonial past.

And are the museums aware of the thinness of the local ice? The Decolonisation targets of speakers at the Queen's-Ulster Museum conference included "the dominance of British rule in Ireland", "anti-Irish racism in Britain" and in the Empire, and "aristocratic collecting", including by the Marquis of Dufferin of Clandeboye, a figure of huge regional as well as international importance.

The colonisation that is in the crosshairs of the RBCM is what we might call doorstep colonialism: the non-native population of the province (including most of the curators) are all products of the British coming to what became British Columbia: to Decolonise is logically to deplore one's own past and present, and regret one's very existence in the province. Surely this is to saw the bough on which one sits? Yet the museum is pressing ahead.

How does this judgement-driven project of Decolonisation in the NI museums intend to address - explain and display - the Plantation of Ulster and the independent Scots settlers? And will the Decolonisation project be accompanied as it is in Canada by Indigenisation? If so, what forms precisely will the latter take? Taxpayers whose Department of Communities gave over £14m in 2018–19, over 80% of their income, to the NI museums, have the right to know.

Let's hope tomorrow's candidate for vilification and cancellation is not the planter in Ulster. (2022)

1   Richard Neal, a Democratic U.S. Congressman, a Catholic Irish-American of an Irish nationalist ancestry, has taken an interest in Irish affairs since the early 1990s.

2   That would almost certainly have been the case had the museum administrators got what they wanted, a brand-new building, in non-European architectural style and costing taxpayers $789 million (the existing style being deemed colonialist). The BC government cancelled the project in the face of public outrage. The Decolonisation project, however, continues piecemeal as the museum re-opens gallery by gallery. (2023)

Sympathy for the Devil?

"Were the DUP right all along?" Tom McTague asked in a recent essay in *Unherd*. This is a question I never expected to hear from the main island of our United Kingdom. The question "Were the Ulster unionists right all along?" would be only marginally less arresting in the wake of Rishi Sunak's Windsor Framework. Yet the thrust of Brendan O'Neill's February 28 essay in *Spiked* is that they were. Mick Hume's downright moving depiction in his March 3 *Spiked* essay of the Democratic and Unionist Party standing alone on the side of the 17 million betrayed angels who voted Leave stunned me. In a half century's touchline observation of events in my home province and cultural forays on to the field of combat, I had heard virtually nothing from the mainland but at best fatigued impatience with, and at worst hostility towards, Northern Irish unionists, never mind the DUP.

So why this Damascene conversion to the DUP and Ulster unionism over the Windsor Framework? Why not over its near namesake the Framework Document of 1995? Or the Downing Street Declaration of 1993? Or the Anglo-Irish Agreement of 1985? Indeed, why not over the Protocol itself of 2020? These were all seen by unionists as united Ireland mission creep or as political grooming to that end. Certainly they were all bricks in the wall rising between Great Britain and Northern Ireland. Is the Protocol not there to placate the Republic of Ireland (and the EU) at the expense of unionism by making official the fiction that there is no international border in Ireland between the UK and the EU and making official the reality of that border between Northern Ireland and Great Britain? Still, though these constitutional milestones were all seen by unionists as relinquishing authority over a part of the UK to the Republic of Ireland, it was before the Republic became the EU's cat's paw during Brexit.

Before any such brickwork, mainlanders hardly thought of Northern Ireland at all in the decades after its creation in 1921–22. It was briefly spotlit with sympathy and gratitude in 1945 when Churchill thanked the province for its part in defeating the German war machine (and was scathing about Eire's neutrality by the same token) but thereafter returned to anonymity. But when it became impossible to ignore the place once British soldiers were sent in 1969 to separate riotous factions (but now in the "legacy" war regarded and pursued by Irish republicans as murderous invaders), mainlanders soon viewed the province and especially unionists with animus. Unionists looked bad and some of them *had been* bad and their bigotry seemed instigatory. At the time, the more hardline among them seemed quite unprepossessing. (To add that religious bigotry in Ireland is mutually reinforcing and has been from when the English and Scots stepped on to the island at least five centuries ago is to engage in the whataboutery that muffles the necessary moral condemnation of specific acts or actors.) But as the IRA terror campaign got under way, what seemed like unionist obduracy (nothing so virtuous as unbowed resistance which surely it had elements of) became embodied in the giant and unlovely figure of Ian Paisley.

Through English eyes, Ulster unionism became synonymous with Paisleyism – evangelical Protestantism with its anti-Catholicism, its working-class loyalist base (with that grating Ulster accent and the Ulster-Scots homeliness, as the Americans would call it), its Cromwellian puritanism, its later opposition to abortion and gay marriage, its endemic rejectionism. "Ulster Says No!" was the cry time and again from hard-faced men as another brick was added. Paisley's roared pledge, "Never, never, never!" still rings in the ears, though hollowly now.

What irony, then, to read English commentators encouraging DUP rejection of the Windsor Framework and even likening such rejection to Thatcher's famous recalcitrance. For them, Ulster Says No! suddenly rings with a tough realism. Yet it was Ulster's unionists, not the IRA terrorists, who attracted the greatest obloquy during the IRA war against the UK. Now Mick Hume tells us (rightly) that the DUP have been "set up as the villain of the piece" by questioning the Framework. But they have always been the villains of the piece, sometimes with justification.

In the twenty-five years since the Good Friday Agreement, and when most tempers had cooled, mainland politicians and commentators had ample time to see the spacious daylight between the DUP and both the moderate Ulster Unionist Party and most Northern Irish, whether they identified as nationalists or unionists. And to see at least the core justice of the DUP defence of Northern Ireland's place in the Union. But they have been unable or unwilling to see beyond the optics on either account. Has this not been a long-standing failure of mainland journalists as well as politicians?

But perhaps the distaste was inherited from the politicians' and commentators' great-grandparents from the thirty-odd years leading up to the very creation of Northern Ireland in 1921–22 in order to prevent an all-island civil war. A creation that acknowledged the growing cultural incompatibility between Catholic Ireland and the Protestant north. At the time of the third Home Rule Bill of 1912, Kipling's resounding poem "Ulster" was premised on the abandonment of the province's cause by Great Britain. The speaker vows that if Ulster falls it will not fall alone. But unionists in fact felt very much alone then and, following the decades of anonymity after they achieved limited self-government, resumed feeling so fifty years ago. But now the loneliness is accompanied by fear and a degree of fatalism as it wasn't in 1912. If political feeling can be part of our personal nervous system, then it is hard on the nerves to be a Northern Irish unionist. For half a century there has been a drip-feed of bad news concerning our citizenship.

It has been a harsh political treatment encouraged by unionists themselves for the following reason: no amount of betrayal by mainland politicians could cause unionists to "rethink" the Union, as one commentator imagined could happen in the time of Truss. Or to rethink unification with the Republic of Ireland. This unshakeable sense of kinship with Britain renders them vulnerable to political sleights and journalistic slights. Having no constitutional alternative can make them resemble an unwanted family hanger-on who out of need will weather all snubs. It even lends them a kind of innocence or naivety (despite their bluster) that seems to invite the very insults that smart.

The contrast between English solicitous anxiety about Scotland seceding and English indifference to Northern Ireland efforts to remain loyal bewilders Catherine McBride in her recent *Briefings for Britain* essay (March 4, 2023) and bewilders all unionists. Even more painful is the English appeasement of Irish nationalism north and south of the island and its tacit encouragement of Irish irredentism, but that is a story for another day. Mainland politicians don't dare insult Sinn Féin but unionists have always been fair game. Thankfully, working-class unionists (i.e. loyalists) have the sense of humour that Glaswegians and Cockneys used to have. When Harold Wilson called them "spongers" they appeared on the streets with orange sponges in their lapels. When Reggie Maudling left Belfast with his plane still at 45° and begged: "Quick, a double scotch, what a bloody awful place" they re-told it and chuckle over it to this day. It was on working-class gables that the inconceivability of unionists joining the Republic of Ireland appeared as the obstructive arithmetic of Irish counties: "Six into Twenty-Six Won't Go", a slogan whose subtext below the wit is that unionists in the event of a united Ireland would not be added to Ireland but would be existentially subtracted in an instant and by definition. Even the cry

"Ulster Says No!" had its comic spawn. I remember watching the 1986 World Cup in soccer in Vancouver on TV with my friend Cormac O Grada when we spotted a banner held aloft by Northern Ireland fans: "Guadalajara Says No!". The allusion at the Mexican stadium was to the Anglo-Irish Agreement of the previous year.

But the successive humiliations have hurt and so has the abiding friendlessness. The Ulster poet John Hewitt in a 1949 poem felt the friendlessness in Ireland that stemmed from the original colonisation of Ulster:

> this is our country also, nowhere else;
> and we shall not be outcast on the world

Surely fear and even despair cower behind the speaker's defiance? The biblical tones are fitting; like the dissenters of Victorian England and the Christians of Paul's time, Ulster Protestants were (and are) "everywhere spoken against". There's been little cultural earthwork in their support since Hewitt. Yet I'm quite sure that identification with Great Britain is tacit in writers of a Protestant or unionist heritage and I wonder if that doesn't create for them unacknowledged personal tensions and repressions.   In the meantime, what a curiously orphaned creature is political unionism.

And in the end it *is* personal. One's self-respect is at stake. The Windsor Framework is the latest among a long series of blows to unionist self-esteem. I have thought to myself in modern English what Enobarbus in *Antony and Cleopatra* says:

> Mine honesty and I begin to square.
> The loyalty well held to fools does make
> Our faith mere folly.

But I suspect that in dealing with the Republic of Ireland on the matter of Northern Ireland, the English are only tactical fools. Besides, like all aware unionists I know Northern Ireland exists courtesy of English taxpayers' largesse, oblivious though many in England must be to that fact. Generosity and obliviousness: am I to be grateful or insulted? I believe unionists are grateful to England (a laughable notion to state-funded northern republicans, on the other hand), despite Wilson's spongers insult; I know I am.

Nor are unionists wont to play the victim card and they may not welcome the tone of my essay. In any case, they have no Great Famine, no Cromwellian atrocities, no Easter Rising martyrs, no "800 years of oppression" to declare in their moral self-assessment return. Nor do they have that potent allure of the Catholic Irish which in the guise of the "native Irish" was first generated by minor English and Anglo-Irish novelists of the Romantic period and was revived by the cultural re-imagining of the Easter 1916 rebellion and has not relented since. Ulster unionists simply cannot compete with this perception of the nationalist Irish, and that perception propels the politics. To this extent the Northern Ireland question is not *au fond* a political problem at all, but one that takes its rise in the realms of optics, imagery, public relations, prejudice, feeling, assumption, reflex, perhaps even by now, instinct. Joe Biden's idiotic attitude to Northern Ireland ("if you're wearing orange, you're not welcome in here"), the Protocol, and to his own "Irishness" is perhaps the sorriest current example of what unionists are up against. Political analysis has abandoned the problem of Northern Ireland to expediency and Pavlov.

English generosity's verso, English obliviousness, can take subtle forms. The title of the excellent Robert Tomb's defence of Brexit, *This Sovereign Isle*, inadvertently explains why the Windsor Framework is blithely contemplated by English politicians. His title ignores the neighbouring isle in order to achieve an understandable patriotic flourish. His title is an echo of Dorothy Sayers' 1940 poem, "The English War" – "The single island, like a tower/Ringed with an angry host" – as though we in Northern Ireland (and indeed Scotland) were not also fighting Hitler from our industrial arsenal.

Reminding the rest of the UK of our existence is exhausting and reduces us to a grumbling appendix. Sayers' and Tombs' imagery convinces me that the Northern Ireland question is more a problem of perception than of politics. Neil Oliver published in 2020 what he calls a paean to Britain. It is a heartfelt and eloquent essay on his sense of Britishness. "My nationality, " he writes, "is a state of mind and I have no intention of changing either. I know who I am and what I love – and what I love is Britain, the whole place, every nook and cranny. This is my island. ... The existence of our homelands is nothing more nor less than an act of will, and also of love… What is truly at stake here, at least for me, is the business of the heart." Every Northern Irish unionist, whose heart-felt nationality, like Oliver's, is British, would second these sentiments though emotional candour is not their currency.

"Long ago," Oliver says, "I realised that the economic argument was not what mattered to me." Nor to most unionists who are far less appeased by the potential economic benefits of the Protocol than alarmed by its catastrophe for the Union. Oliver approaches affinity that embraces the Northern Irish when he writes: "I have also found it unavoidable to see the connections between the character of folk in Liverpool, Belfast and Glasgow on account of shared shipbuilding heritage." But has he assimilated Northern Ireland to Great Britain?

Heaven knows, I'm grateful for Oliver's reference to Belfast, but his paramount concern is the intimacy of England and his native Scotland. Like Sayers and Tombs, it is "the island" of which he speaks, with Belfast and (unmentioned) Northern Ireland as an afterthought. His essay was first published on the UK website, These Islands. But oddly, this site, concerned to promote the cultural affinities of Britain and Ireland, makes no distinction between Northern Ireland and the Republic of Ireland, despite the fact that the latter, as the *Irish Independent* newspaper never tires of reminding its readers, is a foreign country, whereas Northern Ireland, at the time of writing, is not.

In the light of the past fifty years, I'm not naive enough to assume that the rejections of the Windsor Framework and expressions of support for the DUP from these significant mainland quarters have Northern Ireland's place in the Union in the forefront of the writers' attention. But if it is the integrity and sovereignty of the Union that primarily worries them, that is tantamount to the same thing. When Fraser Myers claims in his February 24 essay in *Spiked* that the Protocol in either version "will do nothing to fulfil the Brexit promise of restoring the UK's sovereignty", he is not only reminding us that indeed the devil is in the detail but is also identifying what the woke brigades would call the intersectionality of the matter. The matter embraces the whole issue of Northern Ireland's teetering UK status and its Union-wide implications beyond economics. Kipling's pro-Union speaker's belief that "If England drive us forth/We shall not fall alone" seems eerily apt once more. (2023)

Pretendians

"We are what we pretend to be," Kurt Vonnegut famously wrote, "so we must be careful about what we pretend to be". Lately, several successful Canadians have been told in no uncertain terms that while Vonnegut's premise is false, his conclusion is true and that they were very careless indeed in their choice of assumed identity. Allegedly, and in some cases confessedly, they have pretended to be aboriginal inhabitants of a vast country, with all the overdue privileges their status has recently conferred. Cheyanne Turions was an award-winning curator at Simon Fraser University, British Columbia and recipient of grants intended for aboriginal applicants who resigned in late 2021 after an anonymous Twitter account, NoMoreRedFace, exposed her non-indigeneity. Michelle Latimer is a film curator, actress, maker of documentary films on Indigenous subjects, and TV script writer and director whose series, called *Trickster*, was cancelled in 2021 by the Canadian Broadcasting Corporation when the Kitigan Zibi (Algonquin) Nation denied the kinship she claimed through her mother. Dr Carrie Bourassa (aka Morning Star Bear) was a professor of community health and epidemiology at the University of Saskatchewan who claimed Métis, Anishinaabe and Tlingit identities and ran an Indigenous health research laboratory. She resigned in summer 2022 when the CBC found no trace of indigeneity in her heredity. Dr Vianne Timmons, Order of Canada, Vice-Chancellor of Memorial University, Newfoundland, who claimed Mi'kmaq identity, was removed from office in early April 2023. A CBC investigation could not verify her claim and the Bras d'Or (Mi'kmaq) Nation declined to countenance her. Until August 2022 Gina Adams was an assistant professor at Emily Carr University of Art and Design, Vancouver, claiming to be descended from inhabitants of the White Earth Reservation (Ojibway Nation), Minnesota. A few days after "outing" Turions, NoMoreRedFace posted a tweet accusing Adams of Indigenous identity fraud. Like several of the others, she was a teacher and curator and thus a conduit for Indigenous culture.

The most distinguished casualty of this purge of alleged (white) "Pretend Indians" has been Dr Mary Ellen Turpel-Lafond (aka aki-kwe), Order of Canada, tenured professor of law at the University of British Columbia, criminal law judge, senior counsel with an Indigenous law firm in Victoria, BC, British Columbia's Representative for Children and Youth, and author of a 2020 report on racism endured by Indigenous people in the BC health care system. By late 2022, Turpel-Lafond had vacated these elevated institutional positions after an investigation by CBC News could not verify Turpel-Lafond's Treaty Indian status (Cree Nation), or some of her academic qualifications. Canadian newspaper readers are currently being kept abreast of the serial voluntary return of the eleven honorary degrees conferred on Turpel-Lafond.[1] These high-profile cases involve significant stakes in job appointment, preferment, prestige, salaries and grants. Tellingly or not, they all involve women, but the claims to Indigenous identity made by the well-known Canadian novelist Joseph Boyden have also been disputed. The author of the acclaimed *Three Day Road* (2005, winner of an Aboriginal Book of the Year award among other awards), who has been outspoken on native affairs, has over the years sequentially asserted his Ojibway, Nipmuc, Woodland Metis and Mi'kmq blood. An investigation by the Aboriginal Peoples Television Network (APN) and various researchers could find no evidence for Boyden's claims of indigeneity.

APN exhumed the memory of Boyden's uncle, Erl Boyden, who was the subject of a 1956 *Maclean's Magazine* profile. As "Injun Joe", Uncle Erl in native garb sold fake Indigenous souvenirs to tourists in Ontario and let them take photos of "what they idiotically believe to be a real live Canadian Indian... who am I to spoil their fun?" Erl Konig Boyden's fraudulence belonged to the vanished, more carefree 1950s North America where white tourists could kid around with black bears in Yosemite, having fun with the wildlife and with that other, now tamed forest inhabitant, the "red Indian". Erl presumably didn't go to bed as Injun Joe, despite his nephew's later claim that he had aboriginal blood (Erl admitted he didn't have a drop); there was no transitioning involved here. It seems, however, that in the more serious 1930s, Archibald Stansfeld Belaney did go to bed as his Indian alter ego, Grey Owl, native conservationist and nature writer.

Belaney was in truth a native of Hastings who soon after he emigrated to Canada in 1906 at the age of eighteen, decided to become a Native American, of now Apache, now Ojibway heritage, over the years updating the specifics of his tribal ancestry as occasion suggested. Grey Owl became famous. He received a visit from his admirer, Lord Tweedsmuir, Governor-General of Canada and, as John Buchan, author of *The Thirty-Nine Steps*. He toured Britain in traditional Ojibway clothing (his aunts in Hastings kept mum until a year before their nephew's death), his book *Pilgrims in the Wild* sold enormously, and the well-known writer Lovat Dickson wrote his admiring and credulous biography twice. The truth about this celebrated Indigenous identity fraudster came fully to light only after his death in 1938, and when it did, there was a division of opinion as to the effect on his writings and conservation work. The name Grey Owl vanished from the covers and title pages of his reprinted books, but his good work in beaver protection and forest preservation lessened the obloquy attached to Belaney's memory, a balance-sheet attempted in defence of those currently accused of identity fraud but less successfully.

It turned out that Belaney's duplicity extended beyond the racial self he adopted. He lied about his marital status to a Mohawk teenager and married her bigamously, though she seemed not to care when she found out. When in 1915 he enlisted in the Canadian Overseas Expeditionary Force, he gave his birthplace as Montreal. Later he told Dickson he was born in Hermosillo, Mexico and that his mother was Katherine Cochise of the Jicarilla people (Apache), his father a former scout during the 1870 Indian Wars. Some contemporary identity fraudsters have also had parts of their CV questioned that don't directly involve race.

Belaney seems to have relished the tangled web of his deceptions. Whether that was the case with those currently accused of being Pretend Indians is unclear; likewise, the possibility of their alleged deception reflecting a personal character trait or state of mind. However, their alleged fraud seems more determined and single-minded, less dramatic and alluring; they may be acting a part but they have no intention of adding to the gaiety of nations but only of instructing the rest of us. In role, they are furthering a roughly pre-scripted agenda which, to the extent that they are not actually First Nations, they are furthering by proxy. That doesn't preclude the possibility of some personality trait at work.

*

The agenda crosses the Canadian-US border. Maria Louise Cruz from Salinas, California, despite her Mexican-American background, adopted around the age of 24 the identities of Apache and Yaqui and the name Sacheen Littlefeather. She went on famously (or notoriously), and movingly, to decline on his behalf Marlon Brando's Best Actor Oscar in 1973. The lead actor in *The Godfather* was protesting by proxy the representation of American Indians in Hollywood films and also ongoing events at Wounded Knee, South Dakota (when followers of the American Indian Movement seized and held the town for 71 days). Cruz's sisters told Jacqueline Keeler, a Navajo author, that their family had no Native American ancestry and that their actress sister had fabricated an aboriginal identity for its prestige value. The university historian Liza Black, of the Cherokee Nation, believes Cruz to have been "a troubled woman who made the stories of others her own". Her troubles included an abused childhood and a spell in a psychiatric hospital. She claimed to have been one of the "Indians of All Tribes" (IAT) occupiers of Alcatraz in 1970 but this has been challenged.

Beyond pro-aboriginal rights advocacy, the self-fashioned life of Maria Cruz seemed also to occupy the heady 1960s counter-culture of Ken Kesey's *One Flew Over the Cuckoo's Nest*, American Indian Movement, the Black Panthers, *Black Elk Speaks* and *Whole Earth Catalog* when the American roots of today's woke revolution were put down. It was on the threshold of the 1960s that the journalist John Howard Griffin successfully disguised himself as a black man and travelled for weeks through the segregated Deep South to experience life as a black American. His project borrowed for serious purpose the long tradition of blackface in western entertainment, and his resulting book, *Black Like Me* (1961), recounted the travails of the race he temporarily pretended to belong to. He was supported in his project by the African-American magazine *Sepia*. When the Pittsburgh journalist Ray Sprigle had made the same journey in disguise a decade earlier for his newspaper articles that became a book, *In the Land of Jim Crow* (1949), he was accompanied by J.W. Dobbs, a social leader provided by the NAACP.

By contrast, those recently accused of faking black were enjoying position and prestige in what was presumably meant to be a lifelong project of full racial transition. Nor were new black colleagues privy to their real identity. The two highest-profile examples are Dr Jessica Krug (aka Jess La Bombalera) and Rachel Dolezal MFA summa cum laude (aka Kkechi Amare Diallo), the first a white Jewish woman from Kansas, the second a white woman from Montana of Czech ancestry. Both are clearly intelligent, even gifted and were successful, in the case of Krug as researcher, historian (George Washington

University) and author (*Fugitive Modernities*, Duke University Press, 2018) and in the case of Dolezal as art teacher, university African Studies instructor and activist organiser (rising to become president of the Spokane, Washington chapter of the NAACP). The known Canadian Pretendians share this notable degree of intelligence, education and, in some cases, real talent.

Krug claimed that as a child in the Bronx she had been abused by her drug-addict Puerto Rican mother, a multi-layered fiction recalling Dolezal's claim that she was beaten by her parents, "punished by skin complexion". Rejection of the real parents, and the violent white culture they are held to represent, and the personal victimage thus illegitimately attained, is a common feature of the current race impostor syndrome. Dolezal began darkening her skin around the age of 34, but unlike Griffin, she presumably meant the alteration to be for keeps. By the next year, 2012, she seems to have been accepted by Spokane residents as black. Her father was by then not Lawrence Dolezal of Czech origin but Albert Wilkerson, a black friend. But with Dolezal it was case of the red *and* the black. She claimed to be part-Indigenous, born in a tepee into a family that hunted with bows and arrows. The curious habit among race pretenders of claiming multiple ethnicities is presumably encouraged by life in a multicultural society where one is surrounded by people of various ethnicities. A multicultural society, moreover, that in recent years in both Canada and the USA has become less Caucasian, offering instead a palette of colours to choose from and where whiteness is losing not just its normative standing but its moral standing.

Still, there is a rough hierarchy involved and only certain race or ethnic identities currently qualify, via victimhood, for appropriation. I am an Ulsterman of Presbyterian upbringing and presumably Scots extraction, someone who identifies as British as well as Irish. A satirist aside, no one pretends to be a Northern Irish Dissenter Protestant in heritage. The non-skin colour popularly associated with my heritage is orange (from the Orange Order), though it used also to be black since I hail from what was once called the Black North, inhabited by blackmouths (Presbyterians). In June 1992, the Englishman Patrick Mayhew, Secretary of State for Northern Ireland, met with the Irish Republic's ambassador to the UK. In an aside, Mr Mayhew said to the Irish diplomat, currying favour, that he had "grown up with a detestation of the 'black Protestants' in Northern Ireland." For two generations, northern Protestants have been the last candidate victims for identity theft. Vice-President Joe Biden told the Irish Taoiseach in Washington, greeting him for the St Patrick's Day blarneyfest in 2015, "if you're wearing orange, you're not welcome in here". He cracked the joke (though joke it actually was not) because he knew the Taoiseach had (like himself, or so Joe believes) the politically-correct ethnic identity, i.e. "green".

For over a century, the green has by contrast been much admired and often mimicked. I remember seeing the acclaimed Irish actor, dramatist and impresario Micheál Mac Liammóir impersonating the Irish dramatist Oscar Wilde (himself an inveterate self-fashioner) on the Dublin stage in his one-man show and biggest theatrical success. MacLiammóir himself was in actuality pretend Irish. He was born in north-west London as Alfred Willmore of no known Irish connection, became Michael Willmore when he starting acting, went in 1917 to Ireland to live and became successively Micheál Mac Uaimmhóir, Mac Liaaimmhóir and finally Mac Liammóir. He claimed to have been born in Cork. Like the other "faces", there was a political resonance to Mac Liammóir's greenface beyond the roar of the greasepaint. Mac Liammóir's chosen birthplace, Cork, had republican associations; he became a Gaelic enthusiast when the language was a plank in the pro-independence platform, and with all the fervour of the convert he campaigned for Sinn Féin in the 1918 general election. Since his time and up until today, the superficial allure of Irish identity has attracted the English and Americans to the Irish republican cause, giving it support and credibility which has in effect impeded reconciliation between the orange and the green in Northern Ireland. The effect of Pretendians on Canada's current national project of Truth and Reconciliation has yet to be assessed.

The crossing of ethnic and gender lines has occasionally been a feature of those faking red or black. Rachel Dolezal has been accused by a Gender Studies scholar of spuriously appropriating the rhetoric of transgender identity as well as blackness, of failing to deny that she is "transracial"; in a 2017 interview, Dolezal said she identified as "trans-black". But she has also been defended by a sociologist on the grounds that one can nowadays change one's racial affiliation, be born in the wrong skin and do something about it as one can take on (or liberate) another gender. The alleged parallel between "transgenderism" and "transracialism" suggests a hunger by some for multiple abnormative identities with a history of being oppressed. Such cases might with sufficient media exposure have helped to familiarise us with, if not normalise, the radically diversifying nature of the personal self.

Jessica Krug also crossed the social class line by feigning a belligerent Bronx Puerto Rican persona. But working-class membership is no longer a desirable identity to assume. In the 1930s it was, and in Paris, London and the industrial north of England George Orwell (whom Eric Blair had become) anticipated for social class the race experiments of Sprigle and Griffin. The political implications of Orwell's temporary working-class identity fraud were made clear in the attempts of his publisher Victor Gollancz to muffle the book's reservations about leftist ideology. Recently, however, preoccupations with race and gender in the English-speaking countries have totally eclipsed our concerns over social class and this is reflected in the exclusive prominence of race identity fraud and gender transition claims.

*

The response to accusations of race identity fraud by those accused, and by those whose identity has been forged or plagiarised, might suggest we are living in a crisis of personal identity and by extension a crisis of social and even national identity, with its implications for the cohesion of English-speaking societies. It is rare for those accused of identity fraud to plead mental illness, though several of them have had psychological problems in their background. Jessica Krug in a blog of September 3, 2020 confessed to having lied all her life and to have battled "some unaddressed mental health demons" along the way. It is an abject and almost harrowing coming clean, the kind of self-indictment that reads like an appeal for clemency and forgiveness, and that threatens in its fulsomeness to turn back on itself as self-vindication. But it is also an episode in the decades'-long development of the vulnerable, frangible and often fracturing self that had its relevant origins in American psychotherapeutic vision and practice from the 1960s and that assimilated the notion of victimhood. Innumerable television talk shows, self-help gurus and books, and daytime soap operas advertised the self as commonly abused, oppressed or addicted, while exposing the private self to public view thereby making them one and the same. Indeed, it became a necessary virtue in the world of entertainment and even art to have allegedly suffered. Along the line, this perception of the self was popularly adopted by the other English-speaking societies where what used to be regarded as character flaws or simple bad luck to be weathered are now badges of honour.

A commoner immediate line of defence among Pretendians has been to reply that they were simply believing what they had been told who they were by their elders, usually uncles, parents or grandparents. Boyden, for example, responded to his accusers by citing family oral history as the chief evidence for his Indigenous heritage. In other circumstances, this would be regarded as a flimsy defence, but oral history passed down the generations in aboriginal non-literate society, as anecdote or legend, is taken seriously in Canadian law courts. Genealogical stories are one of three categories of oral history the courts decide on as admissible evidence case by case. Evidence for group rights claims or identity claims (with sometimes vast tracts of land or astounding natural resources at stake) can trump evidence from documentation or even well-known history by the appeal to states of affairs or events "from time immemorial". Moreover, stories of the past are said by some Indigenous peoples to carry incontestable authority. Turpel-Lafond alluded to this when after accusation she was quoted, seemingly still in the persona of an Indigenous descendant: "I was raised not to embarrass, shame or cause harm to families, and not to interfere. ... Growing up, we did not question biological parentage". In this increasingly accepted sense of the past, your personal identity can be interpreted as being what you were told you are (or what you are pretending to believe you were told you are). But Turpel-Lafond may have had a double persona when she spoke: in the non-Indigenous parts of the Anglosphere, my family's story can become "my story" and then "my truth" which by definition is unfalsifiable; so one's race claim could be regarded as one's own truth.

Another defence often made by friends and colleagues is that good works on behalf of a racial cause make racial identity beside the point. What mattered to one of Dolezal's NAACP colleagues was not whether she was black or not but her record in social justice work. But it would be uphill work to claim that her blackness could thus remain intact and that her colleagues should have been happy to have her continue to pass herself off as black. Turpel-Lafond's advocacy on behalf of Indigenous people has been unimpeachable in intention and achievement. But the University of Regina when revoking her honorary degree stated that "her accomplishments are outweighed by the harm inflicted upon Indigenous academics, people and communities when non-Indigenous people misrepresent their Indigenous ancestry". Krug in her *mea culpa* wrote: "Intention never matters more than impact".

But Rachel Dolezal has eloquently defended herself otherwise, on grounds that are familiar to students of postmodernism; what is unfamiliar is the application of postmodernist articles of faith to race here and now. Stephen Greenblatt's influential 1980 study of the self-remaking of one's identity and public persona to reflect current cultural requirements was concerned with England during the 16th and 17th centuries (*Renaissance Self-Fashioning*) but was applied by other scholars to later periods and societies. Greenblatt's work became a tributary of what became, through the later importation of French theory, the mainstream postmodernist claim that much of what we thought natural or historical reality was actually a cultural construct of which we needed to become aware. Criticism in the humanities took the chief form of revealing literary works as cultural construction sites; what was being fabricated were almost always in the service of European (notably British), white, male, colonialist, imperialist efforts at control or supremacy. In our own day, gender not as a natural and an immutable given but as a cultural choice made by the newly empowered self is a contested orthodoxy. The same claim for race ought to have predated the gender claim but didn't, perhaps because the question of race and ethnicity are more collectively sensitive and with a political and occasionally hazardous resonance. Of Dolezal's case, Halford Fairchild, Professor of Africana Studies in California, said that because race is tied to identity politics and not biology, she could appear authentically black by identifying as black.

There is an ambiguity in his observation but not in the quoted opinion of sociologist Ann Morning (author of *The Nature of Race*, 2011) in defending Dolezal: "We're getting more and more used to the idea that people's racial affiliation and identity and sense of belonging can change, or can vary, with different circumstances". Dolezal herself has gone further, stating in 2015 that "challenging the construct of race is at the core of evolving human consciousness". If so, then why not in principle subversively identify as any race you like? After all, the philosophy of multiculturalism has unwittingly encouraged the multiethnic self. In her tactical retreat, after being accused of contriving a Spanish identity, the wife of Alec Baldwin, yoga teacher Hilaria Baldwin (née Hillary Hayward-Thomas in Boston) of no known Hispanic connection but whose talent agency listed her as born in Mallorca, said "I'm a mix of many, many, many things".

And when I became a Canadian, the citizenship judge told the assembly of citizen graduands from 22 countries they were not to leave their previous cultures behind; coming from the divided society of Northern Ireland I thought that foolish counsel. In partial response to that notion of multiculturalism, more cultural enclaves in the cities naturally developed, once European but now because of the immigration policy of the past thirty-odd years, also non-European. These in turn have become "communities" in the recent potent sense and have encouraged the emergence of identity politics.

It was exactly thirty years ago that the Canada Council for the Arts decreed that grants would not be given for artistic projects involving ethnicity of which the applicant was not himself or herself a member. And so the offence of cultural appropriation was born and spread beyond "the arts community"; the policy was retracted but remains informally stronger than ever in the arts world. Multiculturalism was meant to keep cultural differences alive, not dissolve them for a common good, and the policy and goal are known as Diversity. Diversity does not refer to the original ingredients for fusion but rather to multiple distinct identities. Justin Trudeau, whose father was the prime mover of the policy of Multiculturalism, took his father's vision to its logical conclusion when he told the *New York Times* in 2016 that Canada is a brand-new kind of country with no history in the ordinary sense but rather a "pan-cultural heritage ... There is no core identity, no mainstream in Canada"; it is "the first post-national state". He seems to believe he has already successfully decolonised Canada. (The vast province of Francophone Quebec has, however, been encouraged to remain aloof from the diversification imposed on the rest of Canada.)

It would perhaps be odd if some Canadians didn't internalise and individualise this dogma of Diversity. Moreover, the churches, universities and museums now routinely tell white Canadians that their history is reprehensible, even genocidal. Despite its name, the

Royal British Columbia Museum has apologised for its own colonial history and systemic racism and has launched a Decolonisation programme over museum-goers' objections. The Bishop of British Columbia has lengthily checklisted British colonial sins, denounced her own history and observed that BC churches "are places of worship for diminishing numbers of largely white congregations of privileged folks of British descent" (the demeaning use of "folks" for one's parishioners is telling) who will soon be gone, presumably so that the church can leave religious belief behind and get on with the essential work of "food banks and warming shelters, community meals and support groups ... and affordable housing." (The irony is that in a nationwide census 47% of the country's 1.8 million Indigenous people listed their religion as Christianity, but ideology trumps facts.) There has been some pushback against this ideology in the U.S., Australia and the UK but only fitfully in Canada and New Zealand. The alternative to Fight is Flight and perhaps the Pretendians have chosen flight, into the ranks of those who are now championed, not reviled.

*

Yet in this imagined multicultural free-for-all, cultural appropriation is still a dire offence, since there are now innumerable categories of Canadians with core identities (religious, social, cultural) that must be respected, some by law. But the cultural appropriation charge is only levelled against members of what is regarded as the erstwhile Euro-Canadian mainstream which is guilty of forgetting that it is now meant to be a mere cultural tributary. In British Columbia, the British colonising, settling and developing of the province must now be renounced root and branch. (The logic escapes me since it seems a sawing of the branch one sits on.) The knock-out accusation made against the Pretendians by mainly white institutions and organisations that were at first in their corner is that they are keeping alive British colonialism. Revoking its award to Turpel-Lafond and alluding to the notorious residential schools system for native Canadians, the British Columbia Civil Liberties Association stated that "Indigenous identity fraud perpetuates colonial violence and assimilation practices, allowing settlers to shape the future for Indigenous communities while marginalizing Indigenous voices and weakening self-determination".

Certainly there seems something profoundly and exceptionally wrong in impersonating (with personal profit) a member of those peoples who have genuinely suffered in the past, such as black Americans and Indigenous Canadians. But accusations of colonialism seem too blunt a weapon of recrimination. Certainly the Pretendians are "othering" the Indigenous people through impersonation but "othering" was coined to describe hostile activity. Edward Said attacked what he called Orientalism on the grounds that 18th- and 19th-century European representations of the East were very much from the outside and yet were usurpative, a disguised method of hegemony.   But the Pretendians are ostensibly impersonating First Nations people in admiration, homage, at the very least in "allyship", as the current word has it. Such admiration is daily encouraged by the Canadian media, the governments, and assorted institutions: Pretendians took this prescribed attitude into their physical and mental world.

Like others, Michelle Cyca (Cree Nation) in a wide-ranging article on Pretendians in *Maclean's* (September 2022) has blamed the universities and colleges who hired those who proved to be Pretendians for new ways of being colonialist. Responding to the action plan of the 2015 Truth and Reconciliation Commission of Canada, these organisations hastened to Indigenise, meaning at first greatly enlarging Indigenous student intake, adding new courses in Indigenous history and culture, hiring Indigenous faculty and administrators, navigating flexibly around credentials and standards ("lived experience", as Cyca remarks, is now a relevant credential). Cyca accuses the universities of being hasty, greedy (they compete for federal funding), competitive in their virtue-signalling. In this febrile atmosphere, those who said they were of the First Nations were hired on trust as such.

One could clearly accuse the federal government and other social sectors as early as one accuses the universities. Not only in universities but also in law circles Pretendians could flourish. Universities were hasty and careless probably out of fear of appearing racist if they asked for the same level of documentary proof from potential Indigenous hirees as from other applicants. Who is Indigenous? is a question that seems to invite a firm answer (bound up as it is with notions of authenticity and autochthony), with no time for the fluid contrivances of postmodernism or the blithe diversity of multiculturalism. It is the more pressing since through the Truth and Reconciliation project, Canada is well embarked on the long overdue redress owed its native people who are now belatedly seen with justification as our territorial hosts. Much is at stake and the ways are largely unknown. Yet proof of Indigenous status for white organisational purposes turns out to be very complicated indeed.

"Aboriginal peoples in Canada who are classified as 'Status Indians' are registered under the Indian Act on the Indian Register—a central registry maintained by Indian and Northern Affairs Canada (INAC). Status Indians are issued a status card that contains information about their identity, their band, and their registration number". But Cyca qualifies the official definition by reminding us that there are many Indigenous people with living connections to their community who are unregistered as Status Indians. It was perhaps her community activism and connections that led the head of the Union of British Columbia Indian Chiefs to support Turpel-Lafond when the accusations against her were first aired. Indian identity, we learn, is not verified by genetic ancestry. Joseph Boyden published a defence in *Maclean's*, the same magazine that had profiled his uncle, revealing the results of a DNA test showing him to be part Celtic, Native American, Arctic and Jewish. But Dr Kim TallBear (Santee Dakota) and other Indigenous commentators have rejected such broad and contestable categories as criteria for indigeneity. It is solely a question of belonging, of "relationality", of *nationality* deriving from the phrase First Nations. But the tragedy of many Indigenous people is that, as Cyca puts it, "The relationships that constitute Indigenous identity have been deliberately fractured across generations, through residential schools, the Sixties Scoop [the mass removal of Aboriginal children from their families into the child welfare system in the 1960s], and the ongoing overrepresentation of Indigenous children in foster care". Nevertheless, connection is the essential component of true Indigenous identity. But it is not a dual carriageway despite the importance of "lived experience"; it is a one-way thoroughfare. "I am only Cree," Cyca says, "because my kin from Muskeg Lake Cree Nation claim me". There is no such thing as self-identification in Indigenous communities, says TallBear.

But the cases of some Pretendians show the existence of contested spaces, what look like strips of no-man's land. Turpel-Lafond is reported to be a member of the Muskeg Lake Cree Nation through her husband, a former vice-chief and tribal chief of the Saskatoon Tribal Council. Lisa Meeches, an Ojibway TV host and film-maker, announced she intended to adopt Joseph Boyden as her spiritual brother in a traditional ceremony, thus resolving any issues with his ancestry and safeguarding his fiction from possible cancellation.

And what will happen when Decolonisation's twin unfolds throughout Canadian society? In the past several years, to "Indigenise" means much more than affirmative action: in schools and universities white educators take "Indigenising" to mean nativising the whole curriculum, not just creating an Indigenous syllabus. It means nativising pedagogy, educational missions, values and goals, redefining our very idea of the university, even of knowledge itself, in the process cutting down to size anything cultural that derives from British and European civilisation. Canadians are now being told that Indigenous "knowledges, methodologies, cultures, sciences" are epistemically the equal of "western science" (which is alleged to be merely a white branch of science) and "western civilization" and must be taught as such. One expert professor in the field who disagreed has been fired. (My university colleagues now refer to themselves as "settler scholars" to signal the contingency of their disciplines.) Indigenisation is a holistic project that aims to change Canadian places of education out of recognition; arts and humanities departments function in the meantime like social justice institutes en route to some unknown pedagogical terminus. Cyca criticises the universities for requiring Indigenous staff and students "to comply with the institutional ways of doing things. Our inclusion is always on their terms". Given the age of western universities, this compliance would seem for many to be a reasonable requirement, unless structural and procedural changes are to be made on grounds of racial exemptions and exceptions, or, even more ambitiously, which is an emerging proposition, the idea and function of a university are somehow to be nativised.

And outside the academy, in law, mapmaking and placenaming, corporate structures, tourism, entertainment, the arts, museums, all must to some degree be the object of Indigenisation, the positive twin of the negative task of Decolonising. The scale of the project is immense. Billions of dollars are being routed by the federal government to further Indigenising, including the return of huge acreages of unceded land, the transfer of large businesses to Indigenous bodies and the starting up of native-owned business, including tourist enterprises.

The material and economic redress is clearly all to the good and not before time. But the limits of redress have not been formulated or debated. In time the Indigenous forebears of the land could become the exalted figures of the new past and the living chiefs the new Canadian royalty in the event of Canada becoming a republic, since Indigenisation implies the recovery (or creation) of a different kind of nobility and pride. Outside of Quebec (which has been quietly de-Anglicising for years but unlikely to Indigenise; its historic cultural nationalism is Quebec's *raison d'être*), Decolonisation and Indigenisation are a national project that aims to alter the anatomy of Canada as surely as Multiculturalism altered it, and some fusion of the two seems to be the vision of those in power. When the Bishop of British Columbia refers to "this thing we call Canada", implying its illegitimacy, fragility and transience, one might wonder about the shape of things to come.

In the new multiculturalism, the diverse cultures of Canada would be held together not by the Crown or even by Canadian history (both increasingly ignored and equated with colonialism) but by the retroactive agency of Indigenisation. Until that unfolding, the Canadian self will be suspended by the contradictory demands of intensified multiculturalism between, on the one hand, diverse communities protected by the offence of cultural appropriation and, on the other, the new fluidity of transculturalism and transethnicity, both demands sundering most Canadians from their own history.

Meanwhile, Pretendians are those who try, dishonestly, but in a larger picture almost understandably, to self-Decolonise and self-Indigenise inside the Canadian institutions that are pledging to do just that. (2023)

---

1   It was reported in November 2023 that Turpel-Lafond's Order of Canada was rescinded. The most famous Canadian to be accused of Indigenous identity fraud is now the folk singer Buffy Saint-Marie, alleged by the CBC to be of Italian and English stock. She had claimed variously to be of Algonquin, Mi'kmaq and Cree heredity.

Ireland's Belt and Road Initiative

The Arts Council of Northern Ireland has announced that the government of the Irish Republic will fund "all-island arts investment projects" to the tune of £6.4m. These will include turning the historic Bellaghy Bawn in Seamus Heaney's home town at a cost of £4m into "a cross-border residential facility for writers to work and interact". As a literary critic and author of *The Achievement of Seamus Heaney* (1995), I am bound to find this news cheering.

However, funding from the Dublin government's Shared Island Initiative (SII) goes far beyond investing in arts and cultural infrastructure. Belfast and Cork city councils will share £77,000 initial funding for dockland development. Belfast City Council will apply for further money to build a new bridge across the River Lagan from Sailortown to the Titanic Quarter and the Sinn Féin-dominated Council's application will be a shoo-in. BCC has already received £30,000 of initial funding to work jointly with Cork City Council on a rooftop solar heating project, the aim of which is as unimpeachable as that of the Bawn writers' retreat: through renewable energy technology to help decarbonise the cities by reducing dependence on fossil fuels.

Dwarfing these investments is the £38m that will be provided to the University of Ulster to expand their Magee campus in Londonderry. New buildings, an increase in enrolment of students from both sides of the border, a link-up between UU and the

Atlantic Technical University in Letterkenny over the border are what this investment intends to accomplish.

From 2020–2022, over £165m was allocated from the SII fund while £451m is ringfenced for joint North-South projects between 2020 and 2025. According to an August 21 article in the *Belfast Telegraph* by Paul Gosling, author of *A New Ireland: A Ten Year Initiative* (2020), there are proposals to improve the Belfast-Dublin rail connection, reopen the Londonderry-Portadown line with an onward connection to Dublin, and improve the A5 Londonderry to Dublin road, though these are not listed on the SII website.

Although the UK's £10bn annual subvention to Northern Ireland will, of course, remain the essential guarantee of Northern Ireland's financial viability, the SII will allocate a billion euro (£865m) until 2030 for cross-border projects in health, education, the environment, transport, tourism, sport, culture and civic society to interconnect Northern Ireland and the Republic.

Should everyone in Northern Ireland, unionists and nationalists alike, welcome these injections of Irish euro into Northern Ireland? If they are strictly economic benefactions, yes. If they are solely to advance reconciliation between North and South, yes.

And if the Initiative's ostensible aim of strengthening the Ulster economy is solely to help Northern Ireland be a going concern, something I and others have called upon republicans to get behind and that Sinn Féin have never sincerely done, again yes. How could one object?

There is one essential litmus test. Is the Initiative a practical way of advancing the cause of a united Ireland?

To begin with, the overreach of the ten-year Initiative announced by then Taoiseach Micheál Martin in October 2020 turns my green light to amber.

Some of the various sectors of Northern society are to be joined up with their Southern counterparts to their mutual benefit. But some are assumed to have intrinsic deficiencies that need taken care of. Gosling, ex-advisor to the nationalist Social Democratic and

Labour Party, tells us that the Irish government is very concerned that too many NI students are leaving for university in Great Britain, that NHS waiting lists are too long, there aren't enough childcare places in NI, transport infrastructure is weak, and that the Republic aims to fix all this.

If this concern is true, this is hackle-raising to a unionist. These are internal matters for the UK and the UK alone. For example, NI students when they go to a mainland university are going to another part of their own country and it is no business of the Republic's. The NHS is very nearly synonymous with post-war UK. No UK government is inviting itself into the Republic to help remedy any of the multiple problems that beset Irish society.

In the context of this ambitious Initiative, it is important to remember that when we say "cross-border" (a phrase like "across the sectarian divide" that stirs warm feelings in script-writers), we allude to connections between two independent nations, the UK and Republic of Ireland. But in practice these projected connections lessen the sovereignty only of the UK, not that of the Republic.

We are told that the Good Friday Agreement (1998) mandates activities of these sorts. What an Agreement for all seasons it is! No wonder Mr Martin in his announcement hails its "genius". But under "Economic, Social and Cultural Issues" in the GFA, it is the British government alone that pledges to promote economic growth and strengthen "the physical infrastructure of the region". There is no mention of the government of the Republic doing this. To imagine that the "broad policies for sustained economic growth" can be broad enough to involve the Republic by implication or stealth is to give the unionist imprimatur to the Agreement a whole new interpretation.

The Republic's chutzpah is impressive. Gosling reflects Dublin's thinking when he confides that the trick is to get all this done "without unnecessarily annoying unionists" who are the only flies in the ointment of this marvellous scenario. The obstacle is apparently "tribal politics" – not highly justified constitutional suspicion, which is what it is, but just crude unionist atavism standing in the way of all this warm progressiveness.

Martin calls the Initiative "game-changing". So what's the game?

Well, Martin, of the Fianna Fáil party, recently chastised the Northern Ireland Secretary Chris Heaton-Harris for finding unhelpful Varadkar's prediction that he will see a united Ireland in his lifetime. Varadkar was echoing what his Fine Gael colleague Simon Coveney, a thorn in Brexiting Britain's side, said a few years ago. Says Martin: "Since the New Ireland Forum, we in the Republic have always articulated our aspiration to a united Ireland". None of these politicians recognises their predictions (they are not mere innocuous-sounding "aspirations") as significant micro-aggressions or would admit that the Initiative and the predictions are soulmates. And the predictions are attempts at self-fulfilling prophecy.

The Initiative's play is an attempt at what American footballers would call an end-run around the unionists. And around London, though London apparently doesn't care. The Republic's business minister Neale Richmond champions the Initiative to interconnect economically the island *because* he "aspires" to a united Ireland. It's a safe bet that every member of every major party in the Republic thinks alike: Yes to interconnection and to its chief end, Irish unification. Micheál Martin denies any causality in the matter, but who can tell the dancer from the dance? In October 2022, Leo Varadkar when Tanaiste spoke at the pro-unification rally-conference in Dublin organised by Ireland's Future, that future requiring constitutional change, a change with only one real loser. You would have had to come up the Lagan in a bubble not to make the connection.

The northern economy is to be strengthened in order to make the "inevitable" unification a fusion of something more like equals. Have Rishi Sunak and Jeremy Hunt signed up to this scenario?

The ten-year plan is Ireland's Belt & Road Initiative. Via investment and trade, China's B&RI aims to interconnect countries and regions in pursuit of a Chinese-led globalism. The Shared Island

Initiative appears to be its island-sized scale-model.

The SII will invest while all-island trade will develop in the wake of the Windsor Framework which impairs the Union and will subtract a growing portion of NI-GB trade from the NI economy and transfer it to the EU. The ulterior motive of the B&RI is, of course, Chinese political influence around the globe to counter that of the United States. Just as (in miniature) the Republic surely hopes with its Initiative to counter GB influence in NI.

Moreover, I'm quite sure all members of the Dáil regard the island at present as one country, two systems. When the CPP succeeded the UK in Hong Kong governance, they set about fashioning one country, one system to which they had always aspired. Just as they scheme to get Taiwan back, in the teeth of 74 years of separate development. Or in the cases of Northern Ireland and the Republic, 101 years. The irredentist memory is a long one.

In no country can the economy be wholly separated from the country's political structure. Besides, an economy is by nature a fluid thing that also reflects the country's politics in the changing identities of its trading partners. Through the Windsor Framework, as trade between north and south enlarges and diversifies, the Northern Ireland economy will acquire more EU and Irish characteristics.

Nor can the economy be wholly separated from culture. What the careers of both the Good Friday Agreement and Brexit have shown is what the race and gender activists would call the "intersectionality" of our problem. To know Northern Ireland is to understand how Irish nationalists wish the economy, language, education, legality and the past (now increasingly understood as "legacy" and heavily politicised) to intersect dynamically even while they strain between two opposing constitutional aspirations, one far more active and energetic than the other. This intersectionality seems barely understood by unionists but is thoroughly understood by nationalist activists who for the past century have known that culture is the root-system of nationalist politics. For them, the Protocol and the "process" part of the GFA "peace process" are cultural threads of an unfolding narrative. Pursued with determination, there could be incremental cultural and economic changes that cause Northern Ireland to mesh increasingly with the Republic so that over time it fails to be an integral part of the United Kingdom without any border referendum having been taken.

When I read of the Shared Island Initiative, I was taken back to 1994 when Canada lifted its ban on Gerry Adams' coming into the country. The Vancouver Board of Trade hosted a Q & A with Adams and a local panel and I was invited. An expatriate businessman and Fianna Fáil stalwart, who travelled often to Dublin, narrated to me in Vancouver during the Q & A the likely sequence of events as he claimed constitutional nationalists in the Republic saw them.

First we unify tourism, he said, then agriculture, energy, transport and telecommunications – the soft economic targets and infrastructures. Then we go for the sturdier structures and agencies, consent and cross-borderism in the same breath. Fianna Fáil and Sinn Féin grow intimate, Fine Gael and Labour recede. The British don't want you, but we do, he said (a sentiment that is ghoulish to unionist ears). We'll keep 70 seats warm for you in the Dáil. The Alliance Party of Northern Ireland will be the first unionist party through its portals. I told him it was fantasy and he chuckled at my naivety.

As he saw it, it was not to be the Sinn Féin/IRA way but the Fianna Fáil way and the Shinners would finally come on board. Was his take prescient? If the Initiative were to proceed and expand, a border poll may not even be necessary to achieve an ensnaring unification. The Sinn Féin clamour for a Doomsday border poll might come to seem old-fashioned, divisive and unpredictable A successful, open-ended Initiative would rob Sinn Féin of the vengeful poll result they dream of as a party historically wedded to rout and rupture – in short, a Fianna Fáil-Fine Gael end-run of a clever kind.

Since the Anglo-Irish Agreement of 1985, Irish government involvement in Northern Ireland has been recruited to one end. And so far, there is no pushback from the UK, that seemingly doesn't seem to mind if another country (or the EU) has increasing influence in part of its own jurisdiction. From the Republic's perspective, the envisaged political dividend from the unfolding economies of Ireland North and South – unification and Northern Ireland's severance from GB – might appear more winnable than anyone thought before the Framework and the Initiative.

The question is what the response should be of those who stand to gain from Irish generosity yet wish to remain Britons and live outside an Irish republic with which in many respects they are nonetheless neighbours entwined. It would be bathos to suggest that the officials of many countries pondered the equivalent question when the Chinese premier Li Keqiang stepped off the plane. (2023)